VALUE$ELLING

Driving Up Sales One Conversation At A Time

Julie Thomas

VVA
Publishing

ValueSelling: Driving Up Sales One Conversation At A Time
By Julie Thomas

ISBN: 0-9769994-0-4

Library of Congress Control Number:

VVA
Publishing
P.O. Box 8364
Rancho Santa Fe, CA 92067
www.valueselling.com

Printed in the United States of America

DEDICATION

To Team Thomas — Steve, Melissa and Sam

ACKNOWLEDGEMENTS

I would like to thank the many people whose support made this book possible:

Scott Anschuetz, Samantha Barrett-Wallis, J.B. Bush, Sarah Caverhill, John Daut, Dave Kahl, Rick McAninch, Jason McKarge, Keith McLean, Luke Papineau, Tricia Raphaelian, Marty Rowland and Ken Suchodolski contributed their time and personal stories that illustrate the real power of ValueSelling. The entire team at WunderMarx, including Sally Newell Cohen, Jonathan Good, Cara Good and Amy Brandais, as well as Jan King, Gloria Balcom and Christine Frank all kept me on track and were always available with thoughtful feedback, advice, guidance and creativity.

Our customers, sales leaders and sales executives around the world who have used ValueSelling over the years provided me with the proof and reassurance that this pragmatic approach truly does work.

The ValueSelling Associates sales team and our network of associates bring ValueSelling to life and engage customers around the world every day. They are the lifeblood of ValueSelling Associates and are responsible for bringing ValueSelling to their clients. Because of their efforts and tireless work, ValueSelling has had tremendous impact in our client organizations and fueled sales revenue growth and improved sales productivity.

I also owe a debt of thanks to Lloyd Sappington, who introduced me to ValueSelling in 1991 and has been a constant source of wisdom, support and insight ever since.

A special thanks to Cheryl Hallenbeck for all that she does to keep me on track and manage the day-to-day operations of ValueSelling Associates.

Most important of all is my family: Melissa and Samuel who make me smile, laugh and remember what's important in life. My parents encouraged me to go into business and helped me over the years to realize that my passion is in business *and* teaching. Last but never least is my partner in life and business, Steve Thomas, whose constant support, encouragement and patience enabled me to write this book while building and growing ValueSelling Associates.

I hope I have not left anyone out of this process. It would not be by design, rather a mere oversight by me. Thanks to all!

TABLE OF CONTENTS

FOREWORD

I am very pleased and happy to write this foreword for my good friend, Julie Thomas. Julie's thorough and complete understanding of ValueSelling make her uniquely qualified to write this book.

I first met Julie at Gartner Inc. in 1991 when ValueSelling was in its infancy. As I sought to prove to others that the application of ValueSelling tools could enable them to improve their personal sales performance, Gartner was one of my earliest customers. From the beginning, Julie quickly grasped the power of these tools and used them successfully to advance rapidly from sales representative to Vice President of Worldwide Sales Development.

I have watched as Julie took the lead in showing others that the power of these tools goes beyond the theory and understanding. She has a special ability to demonstrate to others how the consistent application of ValueSelling can be the catalyst for long-term sales success.

As one of the first Gartner people certified to deliver ValueSelling training internally, Julie immediately brought a focus to the management of the sales conversation using the simplicity of the ValueSelling Framework.™ Her personal leadership at Gartner caused the worldwide implementation of this method across many different and varied cultures in Europe, Asia and the Americas.

Julie has not only seen the ValueSelling program evolve over time; in fact, she herself has made numerous contributions that have enriched the program over the years. Her intimate knowledge of the core components and the fundamentals of the ValueSelling Framework made her the obvious choice when I decided to sell

ValueSelling Associates. I am convinced that her energy and vision are just the right ingredients to take it to the next level.

Julie understands that in every profession there's always a higher level. Often the best performers are those that learn to apply the fundamentals in a consistent fashion to get the results they want for their customers and themselves. She is committed to helping others get there.

If you've bought this book, in all likelihood you are looking for ideas to apply to improve your own sales productivity. Sometimes it is not even a new idea but a better way to apply what you already know that gets you to the next level. ValueSelling, and the tools it provides, can enable you to more effectively manage your sales conversations, yielding that higher level of performance.

So if you're looking for the way to get to that next level, you've come to the right place.

Lloyd Sappington
Founder and Creator of ValueSelling

INTRODUCTION

Think of someone you have encountered who makes selling look easy. This person may have sold you real estate, insurance — or a complex business solution. No matter the state of the economy and regardless of what product or service she or he represents, people seem to end up saying "yes" to this dynamo.

You may have attributed this success to the fact that this individual is a natural-born salesperson. Well, while having a magnetic personality or being able to tell a good joke can make doing business more fun, these personality traits are not enough to deliver a record of consistent sales success today.

This is particularly true if you are selling a complex, high-end solution requiring multi-level approvals. Take a minute to think about why you chose to say "yes." I am willing to bet that you trusted this person — and that he or she offered you just the right solution for what you needed and wanted. Behind the engaging façade of these "naturals," the pragmatic principles of ValueSelling are at work. This simple yet powerful framework has had an enormous effect on my career and my life and I hope it will do the same for yours.

In 1991, I was a sales executive at Gartner, Inc., the world's largest information technology research and advisory company. I was a successful — and young — sales representative who had been previously trained in a couple of well-known sales methodologies. In short, I thought I knew how to sell.

When Gartner brought in Lloyd Sappington, the founder of ValueSelling, I was introduced to ValueSelling. A couple of things immediately stood out to me. First, it was simple to understand, and extremely intuitive. As a matter of fact, I was already using some of the steps of the ValueSelling process and didn't even know it.

The second thing I noticed was that, unlike many of the sales training programs that I had previously attended, it was tailored to the products and services that I actually sold. Instead of being forced to translate generic process, skills and theory into my day-to-day experiences, we practiced the ValueSelling process on typical buyers with the typical problems and issues that I encountered with my customers and prospects every day. I wasn't practicing the process on widgets and pencils; rather, on the actual high-tech solutions that I sold.

Third, with ValueSelling, being successful did not require a lot of busy work. The process was not dependent on a stack of forms and documentation. Like most sales executives, I found the tedious intrusion of filling out extensive paperwork frustrating and I had no desire to excel at it.

What we are good at is meeting with people ... listening to their issues ... creating needs that may not be recognized ... and linking our products and solutions to the clients' needs. I was excited to find that these skills are the heart and soul of ValueSelling. I had finally found a sales methodology that I could embrace naturally and with enthusiasm.

During my 16-year career at Gartner, I progressed through various sales management and sales leadership positions. ValueSelling continued to be the foundation of my personal success as well as the mainstay of the Gartner sales process. As a manager, my top sales executives were those who followed the ValueSelling process. I took every opportunity to reinforce the training and process, and included it in team meetings. During my first year as a sales manager, my sales team moved from last place in the stack rankings for U.S. performance to a close second place. This complete turnaround was not a fluke, but rather a sustainable change.

In 1999, I was asked to take on the role of Vice President of Gartner's Sales Training for the Americas. My responsibilities included managing a team of sales trainers who delivered ValueSelling to the new sales hires at our company. I also became certified in ValueSelling, and my passion and belief in the process continued to grow. Our new hires included sales executives who had previously worked for companies like HP, IBM and Xerox: companies with great reputations for training. These experienced professionals consistently commented that ValueSelling was the best training they had ever received. It was practical and it worked.

In 2003, it was time for me to make a career change and I reached the difficult decision to leave Gartner and my role as its ValueSelling advocate. To me, it seemed only logical that my next career move should be working for ValueSelling Associates. To this end, I contacted Lloyd Sappington to ask for a job. But I was in for a big surprise.

Lloyd had reached the point where he was looking toward retirement and free time for more golf. As a result, he was actively working on his exit strategy. He was excited about bringing me into ValueSelling — but as the new owner rather than an employee. In stunned excitement, I sat down with my husband, Steve, to review our options. Within six months, and with Steve's total support, we put a plan in place and acquired ValueSelling Associates outright.

Since then, as we have all watched the worldwide business climate become even more challenging, my enthusiasm for the effectiveness of ValueSelling has continued to grow.

The chapters of ValueSelling will take you step-by-step through the basic framework of ValueSelling — from introduction to close — including:

- Why it works

- How simplicity and power are built into the framework

- What you need to know from prospects — and how to ask the right questions to get this critical information

- How to craft the all-important VisionMatch to put you and your prospects on the same page

- Developing true value based on hidden business and personal objectives of the decision-maker(s)

- Structuring a mutual plan that positions you for a relationship-building close

My goal in writing *ValueSelling* is to give you a guidebook that will enable you to benefit immediately from the basic framework of ValueSelling. Then, based on your initial success, I hope you will want to continue to add to your knowledge of ValueSelling. You can learn more about our online and in-person sales training at www.valueselling.com.

I have specifically directed this book to sales professionals (sales executives, managers and representatives) who offer complex, high-end products or services that require multi-level approvals, simply because those sales can be the most challenging. Yet whether your company is large or small, business-to-business or business-to-consumer, selling over the phone or face to face — if you are competing on value and not price — ValueSelling is for you. To succeed, you are competing daily with other highly competitive, confident and passionate individuals.

You must routinely gain and maintain access to busy and elusive executives or senior managers within each customer environment. And because you are often on ever-increasing quotas with a highly leveraged compensation plan, your total income — and your career — are directly related to your sales performance. You are pragmatic and so is ValueSelling.

For those of you who are sales or customer service representatives in less complex arenas, you also will find ValueSelling easy to absorb and highly relevant to your specific business environments.

Before we move into the actual framework of this powerful selling process, I would like to share with you just one of the many stories of how ValueSelling has given a committed sales executive the tools to move to the next level of success.

Karen was a top sales performer when I had the good fortune to become her sales manager. At Gartner, the best sales executives were given an "Eagle" award. Karen had three of these, and had earned her latest Eagle the same year that she gave birth to her second child. Imagine: she was able to achieve this performance in a year that she took three months off of work. She was admired by all of her peers and teammates.

Karen's first year working for me was also a transition year at Gartner because of a couple of significant events. First, Gartner acquired a competitor, DataQuest. The result to the sales organization was that they were now expected to sell a new and very different product line in addition to their core products.

Second, in the middle of the year, the sales leadership team announced that $22 million would be spent to upgrade every sales person's laptop computer with state-of-the-art technology and a Salesforce Automation Application. The catch: in order to fund this technology upgrade, each sales person's quota was raised mid-year.

As Karen's sales manager, I had the "pleasure" of delivering that message. For most salespeople, when their quota goes up their income will go down if their performance is constant. This was certainly true for Karen. She calculated that the mid-year quota increase would cost her approximately $20,000 in future commissions that year. As the sales manager, I decided that we needed to focus on the positive; that it was my job to make sure that Karen and everyone on her team were equipped with the skills, tools and process to be successful.

I quickly planned a team meeting to focus on some "retraining" and refreshing of ValueSelling. What happened next was fascinating to me. You will probably agree that most salespeople hate meetings and will find any and every reason to avoid attending. Karen was no exception to this rule. As a matter of fact, in the past, every time I conducted a meeting, a last-minute emergency had kept Karen from attending.

I published the agenda and announced that we were going to refocus on ValueSelling as the key to our continued success. Karen not only attended the meeting, but during the ValueSelling portion, I noticed her sitting at the edge of her seat. She was completely engaged, taking notes, making connections and creating actions with her current sales activities.

This was amazing to me. But then I realized: Why should sales be different than any other skill-based profession? No one questions that Tiger Woods or Andre Agassi has a coach, or that they are always fine-tuning their game and re-focusing on the fundamentals. The best salespeople, like Karen, do the same thing. They reach out for coaching and training, and also understand that they can always get better.

Karen went on that year to achieve her fourth Eagle and surpass her earnings from the previous year. She attributes her success not only in sales, but in life, to ValueSelling. Applying the process and the formula gave Karen the gift of time. She consistently qualified her opportunities so that she could be more productive in the office and preserve her personal time with her husband and small children.

As it did Karen's, ValueSelling changed the course of my career and my life in a big way. I know that this will have an incredibly positive impact on your sales career and results.

CHAPTER 1:

ValueSelling: The Simplicity and Power Are Built In

"No problem can be solved until it is reduced to some simple form. The changing of a vague difficulty into a specific, concrete form is a very essential element in thinking."

J.P. Morgan, Financier (1837-1913)

We've all had that "a-ha" moment where we realize that winning a sale is not simply about capabilities. Conventional wisdom tells us that the best product or service will fly off the shelves, yet that doesn't always happen. Often, customers will make purchasing decisions using broader criteria: Do these capabilities address my problems? Do they affect my business positively? Are the capabilities aligned with my view of what it will take to resolve the problems? Are these problems worth solving? Does this connect to my personal motivation? Is this product or service what I need?

As a sales professional for more than 20 years, I have had the pleasure of working for market leaders as well as emerging players. I am intrigued by how we win and how we lose sales in the marketplace, and how my prospects have come to their conclusions and made their decisions. While the process is not mystical, decisions are often not made on capabilities alone. It is broader than that.

Recently, I was meeting with a prospect to introduce them to ValueSelling and its impact. The individual was the general manager of the U.S. division of a large multinational company selling optic devices. The reason for his interest in ValueSelling was clear — they had an immediate need to improve their sales results in 2006. The general manager was looking at training his sales staff as a key component to driving sales.

After meeting with him for more than an hour, he requested that I make time for two additional meetings — one with a founder of his division and the other with a top-performing sales manager. Of course, I agreed.

What is interesting is that neither of these individuals wanted to discuss ValueSelling and our capabilities. They were interested in a completely different conversation. They both wanted to know how we helped our clients be successful. They wanted to know how many of our clients had used us for training a second time — not just a "one hit wonder." They also wanted to know how we worked with salespeople who liken day-long training to being locked up in prison.

In other words, how we could actually impact their team was more important to these two individuals than the day-by-day agenda of our training program.

ValueSelling Associates won that business and conducted a very successful workshop. The salespeople, armed with new skills and a consistent process, have significantly increased sales in six months.

The key to successful sales, whether you are selling a product, service or any solution, is in the salesperson's ability to connect to the "buyer". It is our job to help them contribute to the resolution of business issues by resolving business problems with our solution. A complete understanding of their business and their business problems comes before a discussion of our capabilities.

That said, each individual in every prospect you have will justify their decisions differently. ValueSelling is the key to navigating the process, and uncovering and shaping your prospects' views of your capabilities, your value and therefore your ability to win their trust and their business.

It's natural to believe that by simply telling a prospective customer how remarkable your product is and why it's better than anything else on the market, they will then choose you. Many professional sales executives have spent significant time refining their perfect pitch to do just that. But is that enough to be successful? Is just representing the best product in your category enough to guarantee success and significant sales? Not anymore. Over time, prospects — both businesses and individuals — have become more savvy about how and whom they do business with. They are more judicious and cautious about the relationships they cultivate and the vendors they select.

So how do you get a prospect to identify the value you offer in relation to their needs so that they will buy your solutions and capabilities? You begin with a fundamental, yet powerful, concept: Ask, don't tell. It's a simple concept, yet one that's often overlooked.

ValueSelling is a simple approach to connect to the criteria by which our customers will ultimately make their decisions. By executing the steps of the ValueSelling methodology, sales executives have furthered their careers and reached higher achievement than ever before.

The strength in ValueSelling is that it's a sales process that can be duplicated in every complex selling situation: business-to-business or business-to-consumer. It is based on easy-to-learn, repeatable steps that we will detail throughout this book. We will provide you with the tools you need to save time, effort and resources in all of your selling situations, while minimizing the risk of losing the sale or wasting time on those prospects who will never buy anything. You will learn how to quickly diagnose stalled sales, increase your forecasting accuracy, expand each opportunity and reduce discounting. And although the concepts may seem complex at first, the reason ValueSelling works is because it really is a very simple, executable and powerful sales process:

- *Qualifying Your Prospect* — does the prospect have a business or personal issue that you can solve?

- *Connecting the Dots* — can your product or service solve those issues?

- *Asking the Right Questions* — do you have the right information to provide the very best solution?

- *Differentiation* — what makes you stand out from the competition in the mind of the prospect?

- *Developing the Value* — have you clearly connected the unique benefits of your product or service to their specific business and personal issues?

- *Identifying Power* — do you have access to the ultimate decision-maker?

- *Crafting a Mutual Plan* — do you have a plan in place to move the sale forward?

- *Closing the Sale* — Success

ValueSelling is logical and intuitive. So why have we been conditioned to disregard the obvious? To understand, let's take a quick look into the history of the sales profession:

For many years, sales revolved around a prospect approaching a seller in some noisy marketplace. The two would barter — the prospect pushing for the lowest price and the seller for the highest — with neither particularly caring about the value the other received.

In the early part of the twentieth century, a "close the sale at any cost" mentality ruled the profession. Once again, the seller pushed for the highest price, while the prospect fought for the lowest.

In the 1950s, selling moved toward a more enlightened position, one that recognized the importance of the customer's perspective and the value he or she realized from the transaction. By the early 1960s a true evolution had begun: IBM was one of the first companies to introduce the concept of "Application Selling", which focused on the applications of computers in business. During this phase the sales professional assumed the role of an advisor to his or her customers, helping them improve their business operations through the use of the seller's products and services.

By the end of the 1980s, the high-tech industry had exploded, and a plethora of new vendors entered the space: hardware, software, printers; you name it, someone needed it. As all of these new alternatives to IBM entered the marketplace, the new salespeople clearly understood the product and service they were selling. They could speak to the technical issues and solutions, but what they were missing was the ability to articulate why their solution could directly help the businesses they were attempting to sell into.

It was during this period that the idea of ValueSelling began to take root. Lloyd Sappington, who began his career as a sales representative at IBM, became a sales executive at Xerox Computer Services. While at Xerox, Lloyd created his first sales training class, which focused on the value of selling accounting and manufacturing solutions. Although it had its foundations in the applications and consultative selling philosophies, it was focused on the cost justification and return on investment aspects of the sales transaction.

Lloyd trained hundreds of salespeople , and continually refined the sales process he had created to reflect shifting market dynamics. One of the keys to his success was improving the forecasting accuracy of the organization. He began reviewing all of the forecasted opportunities for given time periods and learned that when forecasted business did not close, there were some clear patterns and missing information that were consistently unknown by the sales executives. He was able to identify the five most common reasons sales stall:

1. Lack of Connection to a Critical Business Issue

It's not enough for your company's products and services to be top-notch; they must also resolve your prospect's burning business issues. Prospects who cannot perceive your solution as being connected to a critical business issue will place you at the bottom of their list of priorities, and your sales cycle will probably go nowhere. Many sales executives never bring the business effect into focus, rather staying focused on only solving technical problems.

2. Lack of Perceived Value

Business decisions are typically justified in financial terms and positive business impact. Often sales executives lack the skill to help the prospect uncover the value of the solutions we are selling. Business value accrues to the business issue; in other words, there is no value in a solution unless it resolves a business issue or helps an organization achieve its business objectives.

Just as important as business value is the concept of the individual personal value of each of the people involved in buying decisions.

3. Lack of Differentiation

Our prospects always have alternatives. Whether it is doing business with a direct competitor, resolving the business issue with internal resources or doing nothing at all, seldom are alternatives not in the picture. It is critical that sales executives have the skill to not only understand and articulate how and why they are a different (and hopefully better) alternative but also to create a need for the uniqueness that they bring to the table; thereby locking out the competitive alternatives.

4. Lack of Decision Authority

Sales executives are commonly fooled into believing that purchasing decisions can be made at any level in the organization. In most significant purchases made by organizations today, executive and even boardroom involvement is needed. Underestimating the power that the executives have and the lack of power that middle management often has continues to be a blind spot for many sales executives.

5. Risk

As your prospect gets closer to making a purchasing decision, their personal and professional risk will increase. As sales professionals, we need to remember we are in the risk-mitigation business *and* customer success business.

In 1988, Lloyd retired from the corporate world. That summer, a former colleague convinced him to develop a training program for his sales organization. It was then that he formally developed ValueSelling as a framework to help salespeople link the capabilities of the product to enable some aspect of the customer's business. He applied what he had learned and experienced to create the basic principles, process and tools that have become ValueSelling.

All other sales models focused on the product, or on solving the "pain" issue for your prospects. ValueSelling enables professional salespeople to reach greater success by providing specific, easy-to-understand skills, processes and tools that are simple to implement. The companies that have leveraged ValueSelling have grown exponentially as their salespeople adopted the skills and process and the organization focused on its prospects and customers.

As a sales professional, you already know that in sales, there is no silver bullet; the sales process cannot be conducted in a vacuum. You need a powerful, repeatable framework that leverages how prospects buy. And you must enable your prospects to see the value of getting what they want with the capabilities of your product or service. Great salespeople are in the customer success business.

At some point in your career, regardless of your level, you will experience challenges. I often hear those challenges articulated as, "I can't close the sale." At this point you really need to peel back the onion to determine the underlying issues. The root cause, without exception, can be found through the application of ValueSelling.

No matter what profession you're in, the best always seek to get better. I was fortunate to hear Coach Michael Kryzewski, better known as Coach K, of the Duke University Blue Devils basketball team, offer his thoughts on motivation and coaching. Coach K was assistant coach on the Olympic Dream Team of 1992. Many consider it the best team ever assembled, in any sport, with the world's leading basketball players of the time: Larry Bird, Patrick Ewing, Magic Johnson, Karl Malone and Michael Jordan. When Jordan approached Coach K after a practice, all the coach expected was good-natured ribbing. What happened next astounded him. "I want to work on my offensive moves for half an hour," Jordan told him. "Can you work with me?"

Although Jordan was at the top of his game, and the top of the league, he knew that you don't get better alone and that the time to get better is when you're good. As a sales professional, you're likely reading this book to get even better at what you do by refreshing what you already know or building new skills.

Many of the best salespeople are unconsciously competent in the aspects of selling. ValueSelling brings to even the most successful salesperson a concise framework that builds upon what is already working and provides the tools and skills to be more effective when sales cycles and business relationships break down. It allows you to manage the conversation and move the sale forward by acting as a consultant, rather than a vendor or peddler.

While most sales professionals already consider themselves consultants, there is a subtle but critical nuance that differentiates the two.

Ask yourself this question: When you first meet with a potential customer, what is your primary goal? To tell them about your company and your offering? Or to learn about their business issues and what they currently recognize as needs? Consultants provide solutions to needs and issues. Sales professionals sell products and services. For example, ask yourself: Do you sell PCs (or software or services) or do you enable customer success? If your answer is the former, you need to rethink how you interact with your customers.

In sales situations, it's not about you; it's about the prospect. How can you ever truly fulfill their needs if you don't know what they think their needs are, both professionally and personally? How many slides into a presentation are you before asking a question of the client? If it's more than one, you've probably lost them. Or even worse, if you don't know what their needs are, by keeping the spotlight on your script, you may be giving them a reason not to buy from you. The idea is to paint a backdrop to set the scene for your capabilities. Your props are useless if you don't know the scene.

> *"One of my direct reports had been trying to increase the size of a sale to a large telecommunications company. The sale would result in a longer-term, high-revenue, higher impact relationship with the customer. She had been working hard and doing well, but wanted to get in higher and sell more. She started using the ValueSelling process with each of her contacts. By doing this, she learned that they didn't know the answers to the critical business drivers, or what the company was expecting from the investment.*
>
> *"Her contacts quickly understood the value of answering the questions, and offered to set up meetings with higher-ups. It was a win-win situation: our salesperson was able to make her contacts increase their value to their*

executives by getting to the business issues and getting them into the conversation, AND the sales rep made it further up the chain to the ultimate decision-maker.

"ValueSelling gave us a logical process to get the sales person involved in the conversation. The result was over a half million dollars in additional revenue. And, the client now truly looks to us as a trusted advisor rather than a preferred supplier."

Sarah Caverhill,
The Ken Blanchard Companies

For successful salespeople, ValueSelling is intuitive because it is based on the salesperson's ability to master two keys:

- Interaction with the customer

- Managing the conversation and dialogue

Interacting with your customer should never be confused with "getting along" with your customer. Successful customer interaction entails effectively uncovering their business and personal issues by asking the right questions in the right order and with the right level of depth.

Managing the conversation with your customer is critical. Yes, you have to have a strong pitch, but the key is to connect with the customer's perspective rather than expecting them to connect with yours.

One of the most powerful subtleties of ValueSelling is the premise that, "It's not about me." It is about unlearning the "tell" mode and shifting the spotlight to the prospect and his or her view. To do this successfully, you must ask good questions and listen to the answers.

You manage the conversation through your questioning techniques. As David Kahl, former ValueSelling client and current ValueSelling associate, explains, "You need to allow the prospect to talk, because when we turn the spotlight on them, we make them do the heavy lifting. When the focus is on you, you do all the work by trying to continually move the conversation and rarely get the true information you need."

Success doesn't simply rest in the specific questions you ask, but rather in how you conversationally ask those questions to obtain the specific information you need. The objective is to move the prospect through their buying process effectively. We often demonstrate more credibility and value to our prospects and customers through the questions we ask than the answers we give.

Each chapter in ValueSelling focuses on specific strategies to move the sale forward. We'll dissect each element of the ValueSelling process and provide you with the tools you need to:

- Create a need for your differentiation
- Connect the value you bring to resolving the customer's critical business issue
- Uncover and connect to the prospect's motivation
- Establish the business case and justification
- Identify, gain and maintain access to the ultimate decision-maker
- Craft mutually-agreed-upon plans with specificity so that you're working together toward a single objective and timeline
- Pull it all together so that you can shorten the time it takes for your customers to act and increase your productivity.

CHAPTER 2:
The Foundation of ValueSelling:
People Buy from People

"Success is neither magical nor mysterious. Success is the natural consequence of consistently applying the basic fundamentals."
Jim Rohn, Motivational Speaker and Entrepreneur (1935-Present)

As an experienced sales professional, you already know that the business climate has changed profoundly in recent years. Enron, Tyco, Halliburton and other corporations are the most notable examples of consumer and shareholder deception. As a result, accountability, trust and ethics are key.

Trust is simply more difficult to establish these days. People are wary and cautious. After all, *everyone* has been burned at one time or another by a salesperson who promised the moon but never delivered. Remember "vaporware"? Vaporware is software or hardware that is publicly announced or actively marketed (often to influence prospects to put off buying competitors' products) but which has not yet been produced. Oftentimes, the product is never produced, is very late to market or never lives up to the marketing and sales promises.

The examples I mentioned can and should be blamed on the executive suite. So why do sales executives get a bad rap? Often, the prospect doesn't believe the sales executive has their vested interest at heart. They believe that your success is at their expense. What's true in real life is true in business relationships: You place your trust in those who you believe will not hurt or take advantage of you.

While price and capabilities are and will always be important to the equation, customers are increasingly looking for partners who have the same values, can be trusted and are accountable. From a customer's perspective, salespeople ARE the company they represent. Therefore, a successful sales relationship hinges on the personal relationship you develop with your prospect. The greater the trust and rapport, the easier it is to encourage your prospects to share their personal motivation and to discover how your products can create value for them and their businesses.

As buyers, we all are more likely to trust someone who demonstrates expertise, professionalism and an understanding of our needs; someone whose behavioral style is similar to our own. It's human nature. But more important, we trust people who demonstrate an understanding of our problems. Furthermore, we're willing to engage and invest time and energy in conversation with these people. This is a fundamental principle upon which the ValueSelling Framework is built: People Buy from People.

The best salespeople are those who realize that you can never force a person to change because you think they should, or force them to see what you see. Successful salespeople are able to re-engineer the customers' buying process and effectively navigate through their process rather than force the customers into their process. So how can we help the customer through their process and ultimately facilitate their choice of our solution? To create and maintain rapport we have to begin by understanding the customer.

The foundation of ValueSelling is based on six logical principles that are truisms of how sales professionals and buyers interact.

Whether you're trying to get your foot in the door with a high-level executive or a mid-level manager, your ability to succeed lies in understanding and applying these basics:

FUNDAMENTAL PRINCIPLES OF THE VALUESELLING FRAMEWORK

People Need a Reason to Change

The Product is in the Mind of the Buyer

People Make Emotional Buying Decisions for Logical Reasons

The Correct Use of Power Is Key

You Can't Sell to Someone Who Can't Buy

FOUNDATION PRINCIPLE: PEOPLE BUY FROM PEOPLE

PRINCIPLE 1: People Need a Reason to Change

The idea that people need a reason to change is the most basic and obvious of concepts. Change is difficult for many people: It includes risk, uncertainty and the likelihood that they are going to have to put in long hours and effort to successfully manage the change.

Think of it this way: For an airplane to take off, it needs a tremendous amount of thrust, but once the plane is up in the air, the pilot can power down. The same is true in our sales situations: It takes energy and hard work to make a change, but if it's done for the right reasons and there is issue alignment and resolution, it will take less energy and work to maintain the change.

As a salesperson you cannot force the customer to change. If that is your approach, you will likely lose and be very frustrated in the process. You need the customer to own the idea by first guiding them to identify their issues and uncover the reasons they need to change. A prospect must then see enough value in addressing their reasons for change to motivate them to want to become a client or customer of yours.

A top salesperson whose company had implemented ValueSelling once told me about the time he was working with a prospect to sell a substantial automation equipment purchase into a health provider. The prospect was a 29-year materials management veteran who was just one year away from retirement. The sales executive had been using the ValueSelling formula throughout the sales process, and thought that he completely understood the prospects business issues and requirements: He asked the right questions, understood the business issues and proposed what he felt was the best solution to meet the prospect's needs.

At the end of his presentation, the prospect informed him that while he offered exactly what he needed, the cost was too high for him to justify. He was honest in telling him that, ultimately, he didn't want to expend the effort it would take to incorporate the system, or rock the boat with only a year left before his retirement.

Understandably, the sales executive left the meeting dejected, yet obsessed with trying to figure out how to turn the situation into a win. All of the sudden it occurred to him: He knew that that the prospect was retiring and would most likely rely on his former employer for long-term healthcare in his golden years, so he called him back to ask one question: "I respect your feelings, but since you're going to retire and live locally, who's going to fund your healthcare moving forward?" To the sales executive's relief, it was the company the prospect worked for. So he asked the next question: "Wouldn't you want the healthcare provider you choose to provide the very best in benefits long-term?" The answer was a resounding yes. He had found enough personal value that could move the sale forward.

He had reached a stall. But by using and applying the ValueSelling Framework, he was able to determine that his prospect was risk-averse in terms of workload and fear of making an error that would ruin his legacy. The sales executive was able to overcome this obstacle by using that same risk-aversion as a positive motivator. And he learned a valuable lesson: Most people will spend more energy doing things to avoid looking bad rather than take the time to look good and succeed.

To convince a prospective client that change is needed, you must be able to resolve an issue. It doesn't matter if you have the best widget or solution if all you have is a solution in search of a problem. Our goal in connecting to a reason to change is to connect to something that is bigger than simply solving a problem or eliminating a nuisance.

There are two clear motivators to making change:

> Business Issues — Business goals and objectives
>
> Personal Issues — Individual goals and objectives

There is a distinct difference between key initiatives or goals and business issues. A business goal or, stated another way, a business objective, is what customers need to accomplish maintaining or growing their business. A business issue is something customers need to address and resolve to achieve their objective. Once that issue is identified, you drill down for a problem to solve — a difficulty that prevents your prospect from being able to satisfactorily deal with or resolve their business issue. Whether you are coming in with a new solution or trying to displace an existing vendor, if you cannot uncover a reason for change, neither will your prospect, and nothing is likely to happen.

Timing is everything when you're probing for a reason to change. You may have been trying to get in to see a prospect for months, or even years, with no success. All of a sudden you hear from him. Why? Something must have changed in his world or perspective that makes it timely to discuss your offering.

But once you uncover that issue, it opens the door to craft your solution and uncover your unique value. The only thing that matters is the customer's perception of the value or effect of being able to resolve his business issues.

Here's a great question to ask yourself when you are identifying the need to change: Would they use my product or service if it were free? You can have the best product available, but if customers don't understand and connect with the business and personal issues, they won't buy, or take it even if it is free because they don't see the value.

PRINCIPLE 2: The Product is in the Mind of the Buyer

It doesn't matter what you do — it matters what the prospect thinks you do. Taken a step further, it's not what our brochures say, it's what we know will fit in with the customer's requirements. It's the work we do to really bring what we do to life for the customer that makes it easy for our prospects to do business with us.

Put it into your own perspective: When you buy a house, for most of us the single largest purchase we'll ever make, you're not buying the walls — you're buying the neighborhood, the schools, the location, the architectural style — you're visualizing your own unique life in that house. More simply said, no matter what the purchase, no two customers will ever see it or visualize it the same way. They'll envision it based on their own issues, context, history and perspective.

It's no different in business. You make purchases based on what you think that product will do for you. This is one of the characteristics of a good salesperson: the ability to identify exactly how the customer anticipates using or experiencing your product or service, and to shape the customer's perception of the product.

One of our own ValueSelling associates recently relayed a situation that illustrates this point. J.B. Bush was asked by a customer to validate a large opportunity that was forecasted to close that month. It was considered a "must-win" opportunity for the company. When J.B. arrived at the customer site, he found a team of eight, many of whom he had not met, ready to discuss the sales situation.

> *"The Global Account Representative and the local*
> *account representative quickly went into presentation*
> *mode, attempting to convince me that this deal was*

closing as forecasted. I sat back and patiently listened, asking a few confirmation questions along the way, getting a feel for the structure of the proposal, the steps they had taken, and the resources committed. When they completed their presentation, they sat back, grinned at me — one guy gave me a thumbs-up sign while another actually winked at me as if to say, 'we nailed it, didn't we?'

"*Then I started to ask them a few questions that were intended to reveal what information they knew from the customer's perspective and how well they were aligned with that perspective and had confirmed that with the prospect in writing.*

"*I quickly came to discover that their presentation was great-looking, polished and professional; many resources had been used (including senior executives' time) but ...*

"*They were unaware of the customer's view, and thus could not confirm that they were aligned with the customer's primary business issue. They could not articulate and confirm that the prospect was convinced of their differentiation. As a matter of fact, the sales team had told their sponsor within the prospect what the value/impact was going to be on the business.*

"*It was very likely that a disconnect existed between the prospect's view of their issues, problems and solutions and the sales team's perspective.*"

You know what happened? The deal did not close as planned, and was delayed over six months.

Salespeople often run into the trap of not understanding what their prospects do or don't understand. To be most successful, it is critical to connect to and confirm that their understanding is complete, in their language. As salespeople it's our job to create and confirm that understanding in their mind.

Have you ever had a situation where the prospect tells you that they know all about your company? When they tell you this, you need to confirm that this is true by asking them to explain it to you.

They may even be willing to buy something from you. Maybe they are right — but what if they are wrong? What if they are buying the wrong solution or have outrageous expectations?

In ValueSelling, we define **Business Issues** as those concerns that prospects need to address and resolve in order to achieve their business objectives. The key is that your prospects must envision the capabilities of the product or service you offer in a way which enables them to solve their problems better than any other alternatives, thereby resolving a key business issue, and helping them achieve a key business objective.

In the ValueSelling Framework, this process of connection is called **Creating a Differentiated VisionMatch.**

PRINCIPLE 3: People Make Emotional Buying Decisions for Logical Reasons

A common misconception is that an emotional buying decision equates to an irrational buying decision. This is absolutely not the case. An emotional buying decision means that you're connected on a personal motivation with the individual making the decision.

It's identifying what gets their heart beating, their adrenaline pumping and them motivated to act.

People are motivated for their own reasons, not ours. Remember the earlier story about the executive one year away from retirement? The salesperson was able to get over the risk-aversion by focusing on his prospect's individual concerns about long-term health care. That provided the motivation for him to take on an additional workload and overcome his fear of failure. Did he make a bad decision on the company's behalf? Absolutely not — the business value was there — they bought world-class systems and realized a tremendous return on that investment.

Salespeople who are effective at connecting on an individual level are more successful throughout the sales cycle. It is important to note that understanding the emotional issues is not the same as delving into one's personal life. It is investigating and connecting with the motivators and aspirations of the people we are working with.

Value, whether perceived or real, tangible or intangible, is the heart of motivation. We have to connect with their perception of the benefits and impact of our solutions. It is the prospect's perception of the impact our solution will have on their business. People will buy something if they believe it has both business value and personal value:

> **Business Value:** Your product must provide measurable impact to the prospect's business, such as Return on Investment (ROI) or cost savings. Value accrues to the business issue and is customer-specific.

Personal Value: You cannot make a sale unless you satisfy a prospect's personal reason to change or act, also known as the "What's In It For Me," or WIIFM, factor.

The more effectively you help your prospects connect the value in your solution to their business and personal objectives, the stronger their motivation to take action with you. It is critical to think about your prospect on two levels: We want the organization as well as the individual to be successful.

PRINCIPLE 4: The Correct Use of Power Is Key

Everything that we discussed so far is for naught if it is not with the person who has the authority to make a purchase — or who has **Power**. Until you have access and insight to the Power Person's view on their business issues, solutions and value, you are at risk that they see the world differently than you. And equally important, if you aren't selling to the person who can buy, your time may have been squandered.

It can be more difficult than ever to determine who actually has this authority in your prospects. There can be many reasons for this:

- The person who you do have access to tells you they have authority to procure and may even believe that he or she does

- Some salespeople assume that if someone is willing to meet with them, or be their sponsor, they are the power person

- Some salespeople don't have confidence that they can provide value to the executive and self-sabotage themselves by not even trying to call higher in the organization

Self-sabotage can be a huge barrier to winning the sale, whether it's a fear of having nothing to say to someone in power, or a fear of looking stupid. In reality, the higher up you go, the easier it often is to have a business conversation; it's all about business/bottom line and less about technical specification and details of your solution. However, you may only get one chance to get an opportunity to sell starting at the top — you must be prepared with research so that you can ask good questions, and learn about the executive's perspective and agenda.

At the end of the day, if you don't have the power person, you're at risk of wasting time and resources on opportunities that will not close. Implementing and applying ValueSelling is about mitigating risk. The most effective salespeople establish and maintain rapport at the power level, i.e., with the person who has ultimate authority to sign off on a purchase or allocate funds to implement a project. To make the sale, it is crucial to have a VisionMatch between you and the Power Person.

At the same time, our prospects don't have all of the power in this interaction. Sales professionals have power as well and must use it wisely. How you spend your time, allocate precious resources from your company and negotiate all through the sales process is your correct use of power.

PRINCIPLE 5: You Can't Sell to Someone Who Can't Buy

Simple isn't it? Yet how many of us waste precious time and resources developing a prospect with someone who doesn't have the authority to buy. There are all kinds of reasons to call on people who can't buy. Until we identify and gain access to the person who can, however, we are at risk. We may get lucky! Yet our goal is to be successful because of our efforts, not in spite of them.

All of these issues become the basis for developing your prospect and determining if the sales process will proceed. By using the ValueSelling questioning process and strategies that you will read in the next few chapters, you will be well equipped to make the sale.

How One Company Avoided the Bidding War

HA-International serves the North American foundry industry as the largest supplier of products for core/mold production. The company offers the most comprehensive range of products supported in three market segments: Resins Systems for bonding sand; Resin Coated Sand for the shell process; and Refractory Coatings.

HA-International was formed through a joint venture between Delta Resins and Borden Chemical in 2001. The sales cultures of the two organizations were significantly different. One group was selling on price; the other was selling on price *and* value. The window of opportunity for resin coated sand products is relatively small, with only approximately 2,000 possible customers in the U.S. at any give time. Because of this, the company was experiencing eroding margins and high competition, quickly forcing it into a commodities business. Customers were pressuring suppliers to contain costs. While HA-International offered a superior technology, it wasn't being perceived as unique enough to demand a higher price.

HA-International needed a consistent, repeatable methodology that would enable its sales team to sell based on the intrinsic value the company's solutions bring to its customers. The sales team needed to be able to understand their clients' organizational issues and challenges so that they could articulately differentiate their products, solve the customers' true needs and act as sales consultants, building long-term relationships based on value rather than cost-cutting.

By using the ValueSelling Framework, HA-International was able to arm its sales team with the skills to manage the dialogue with their prospective customers in ways they had never been able to. By focusing on the need to learn their prospects' business issues, the sales team members were able to identify and differentiate the unique value of their products in solving their prospects' needs.

As a result, HA-International's margins increased 20 percent from the previous year. Account penetration also increased significantly, contributing well over $1 million in bottom-line net margin. According to Keith McLean, president of HA-International, "It is the most successful year we've ever had. The sales team is talking value, and my phone never rings anymore with salespeople trying to compete on price. And while we've been growing the business in volume, it isn't at the cost of margin."

As HA-International's success illustrates, trust and rapport are essential in encouraging potential prospects to share their challenges and allowing you to participate in crafting your value-added solutions. Therefore, your ability to create — and maintain — trust and rapport is critical. In order to do this, you must win your prospects' confidence by knowledgeably dealing with their questions and concerns, and by professionally managing the relationship. When this happens, prospects come to the table with increased confidence in you and willingness to continue to work with you.

Sales professionals who excel in establishing trust and rapport stand out from the crowd and take both their prospect relationships — and their sales commissions — to higher levels.

ValuePrompter

How to establish trust and rapport:
- Respect your prospect's time and deadlines
- Listen empathetically and confirm feelings
- Demonstrate knowledge of your prospect's business
- Establish a shared understanding
- Deliver on promises
- Be accountable for you and your company
- Respond in a timely fashion
- Project authenticity

Here are the concepts you can apply today to escalate your sales performance:

- *People Need a Reason to Change* — A prospect must believe there is sufficient need to change before he will become your client. To motivate him, you need to guide him to identify his issues and uncover the reasons they need to change first.

- *The Product is in The Mind of the Buyer* — Prospects purchase based on what they think your product or service will do for them. You must help them identify exactly how they anticipate using or experiencing your product or service, and shape their perception and understanding of your offering in a way that is better than any other alternative.

- *People Make Emotional Buying Decisions for Logical Reasons* — Prospects will buy something if they believe it has both business value and personal value. Help your prospects connect the value in your solution to their business and personal objectives, and they will be motivated to buy.

• *The Correct Use of Power Is Key* — If you don't have access to the person who has the authority to make a purchase, you're at risk of wasting time and resources on opportunities that will not close. Mitigate the risk by establishing and maintaining contact with the power level so that you can learn about the executive's perspective and agenda.

• *You Can't Sell to Someone Who Can't Buy* — Until you identify and gain access to the person who can buy, you are at risk. Develop your prospect through questions that enable you to determine if there is a need, and whether the prospect is committed to making a change based on his business and personal issues.

CHAPTER 3:
Connecting the Dots for Your Customers

"What concerns me is the not the way things are, but rather the way people think things are."

 Epictetus, Greek philosopher (A.D. 55-C.E.135)

Have you ever wondered why a deal didn't close?

In more than 20 years of experience working with hardware, software and service companies, I have repeatedly witnessed the truism that approximately one-third of all sales cycles come to an end with no decisions having been made.

The most expensive outcome of a sales cycle, and the one that wastes more resources than any other, is the one that ends in "no decision". If you could eliminate your "no decision" sales cycles, you could improve your productivity by as much as 50 percent.

Can you imagine virtually eliminating the "no-decision" factor in your sales pipeline? No single selling skill can have as much influence on increasing your close rate than prospect qualification.

> *"I got a phone call one day from a former employee who was looking for a reference. I agreed, and two weeks later I got a call from a software company in San Diego. We talked about the former employee and how he focused on doing the best job he could.*

"It was during the call that I realized that I should use the sales qualification process to sell my friend. I began asking about their business issues. I learned that the woman was a new VP of sales for a company that intended to be bought or go public. But because they sold solely through third-party distributors, they weren't making the right numbers, so she immediately had to hire a direct sales team and ramp up sales to show immediate revenue growth.

"I put on my own salesperson hat and asked, 'Is it going to be a problem to hire all these people with different backgrounds, using different sales methodologies?', 'As a manager, is it going to be difficult for you to communicate your company's value proposition to your team so they can sell that value to prospects?' I was trying to expand her thinking about her issues. I then asked, 'What do you think you should do?' She said, 'I think I should hire a sales training system.'

"There it was. So I asked if I could tell her about what I do, of course focusing on the speed of ramping up by using ValueSelling. She wanted to use us, but had no budget. So, we developed a plan: She provided access to Power, and would secure a budget if I would sell our service to her power people. Six weeks later I was typing up the invoice. The key is that you have to understand the business issue whether you're on their radar or off it."
     Rick McAninch, ValueSelling Associate

Although Rick's original intention was to help his friend land a job, he quickly accomplished the two key elements to qualifying a prospect:

- Confirmation between yourself and the prospect of their unresolved business issues and the unique solution it will take to resolve them

- The perception of the value of being able to resolve their business issues

As Sarah Caverhill of The Ken Blanchard Companies explains, "The qualification process is extremely valuable. It takes the conversation to a completely different level that enables you to categorize what you know and figure out what you don't know, but need to."

Your mission is to help your potential customer connect the dots in their own language. To do this, you have to determine what it is that drives them, and the only way to understand this, and adopt their language, is by getting them to define the business and personal issues, not just the problems that they are trying to solve, so that you can drill down to the true value of your solution.

It begins with a business issue, something prospects need to address and resolve to achieve their business objectives. While you will often hear from a prospect that their issue is to increase revenue or reduce expenses, don't confuse objectives and issues. Objectives are goals. Issues relate to tactics. Business issues are generally caused by any number of problems that prevent prospects from being able to satisfactorily address or resolve their business issues. Solutions are anything — products or services — that can eliminate the problems and resolve those business issues.

At the end of the day, people don't like to be sold; they like to buy. And as a successful salesperson, your job is to help them buy. The challenge for sales professionals is that customers now expect us to fit into their process, not the other way around. They are more savvy and less dependent on vendors for education, yet expect more in terms of linking the impact of your products and services to their business issues.

Whether it's resin-coated sand or high-end software, they are asking you to help them answer the following questions: Can I buy? Should I buy? What's the effect to the company, and my career? It is your opportunity to qualify them as a prospect while they are qualifying your product or service.

Prospect qualification goes far beyond assessing whether they can buy. It must also include determining if they can buy, should buy, and most important, if they will buy.

We've reverse-engineered the process of how customers make big-ticket purchases, so that you will have a 50,000-foot view of the basic steps people go through and how you can successfully help them navigate. Either consciously or unconsciously, each of your prospects goes through the following ValueBuying process before making a decision:

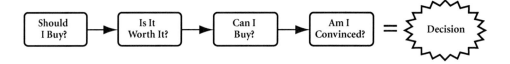

How Customers Buy

Should I Buy? Does the prospect have a burning issue that needs to be resolved? Every business has them and every business makes investments to solve those issues; it could be purchasing needed systems, hiring additional staff or building. Such investments are made for the sustainability and longevity of the business. Once your prospect tells you about his burning issue, you can identify the root cause: are they technical issues, supply issues, capital issues? The root cause is the problem that you need to solve.

Understanding all of the elements will help you answer the question "should I buy?" From a sales perspective, it's the challenge to uncover the elements that you are uniquely qualified to address in order to create differentiation.

Always keep in mind that there are lots of products out there that a customer shouldn't buy. Just because there is the promise of ROI doesn't mean the customer needs it to sustain longevity.

Once you've established the true business issues, you are able to look for the solution that matches to the customer's view of how the issue can be solved.

Will I Buy? If I am able to solve the prospect's business issues, will it be worth it to them? What your prospect is pondering is whether it is worth the effort and the expense to solve the problem. Can they justify it and will the company find value? A great way to look at this is, would you spend $9 to make $10? For most of us, the answer would be no, but every business and individual has a different gauge of what's valuable or worth it. We all view this question differently based on our own perceptions and experiences.

Say someone gave me and my assistant Cheryl $10,000 each to spend however we chose. I'd likely go to Africa to recharge my batteries, because that's what is valuable to me, but Cheryl, on the other hand, would undoubtedly spend the money to work on her house. This is a customer-specific question, and there's no easy answer.

Can I Buy? Have the two questions been answered by the person who has the authority, the research and the courage to buy? We know that they won't always buy even if they see the value, because they can't. You want to find out if they have the capability to purchase. In today's sales, that person is often is hard to find, or may be diffused throughout the organization. Approval levels have risen two positions in the past few years in order to protect people from making mistakes, and to protect the company from ill-advised spending. In other words, that same mid-level manager you sold directly to just a few years ago now needs approval from two people above her to make any purchases. Consequently, these two people must also be educated — and sold — on the value of your products or services.

Another important aspect of resolving the question of *Can I Buy* is: *How Risky Is This?* How much value does the prospect place on solving their business issue? This requires an assessment of the value you prospect places on using your solution to solve that issue. The value must be great enough to motivate the prospect. Companies and individuals both have risk-tolerance. Any change carries with it a risk. You must uncover the prospect's true willingness to enact a change and confirm their perception of the company's willingness to do the same. Sometimes what comes out of it is that you learn the person you're working with isn't the right person. This is the step to mitigate your risk in the future.

While I was a sales executive at Gartner, we talked about personality types A, B and C. Type A is the front-runner and risk-taker — 50 percent of their plans failed. Type B is more in the bell curve — they'll take it on once it's proven to succeed. Type C is the complete laggard who will only move to new technology and practices by dragging his feet. Ideally, you want your prospect to be an A. The B personality can be persuaded, but the last thing you want your prospect to be is a C. If you're a widget company with the latest and greatest product, but you go approach an old-time manufacturer to buy your new widget, you should know from the start that they'll be the last to come on board. Determining their perception of risk by qualifying them will mitigate your own risk.

Resolving each component in the ValueBuying process is critical to your ability to differentiate your offering and ultimately close the sale.

The Perception of Value

The second element of the prospect qualification equation is Value. We define Value as the prospect's perception of the impact of your solution in resolving the business issue, in other words, whether or not there is enough value to move forward with your solution. This impact must be expressed in terms of both business value and personal value. In an ensuing chapter, we will explore the difference between business value and personal value and why both are critical to developing a qualified prospect. We will also look at how you can leverage value to create urgency and motivate your prospects to act.

Value is both micro and macro. You need to understand the value on a business level as well as an individual level. Two people might make the same procurement decision based on two very different levels. For example, what if your product was a laptop computer?

There are a variety of benefits in purchasing a laptop instead of a desktop computer: portability, reliability and cost savings are just a few. From a business perspective, a laptop and desktop are virtually equal in terms of maintenance and the ability to network across an enterprise. One prospect could buy the laptop for its portability, while another might choose it based on its reliability. Micro-value is really the tie-breaker in such purchasing decisions. If you have two products with equal business value to choose from, then purchasers ask themselves which they are more comfortable if all other issues are equal.

Tying It All Together

By now you are likely starting to see how ValueSelling coalesces into a cohesive sales methodology. By resolving the issue of value, and delving into the prospect's buying process, you also satisfy the ValueSelling Principles:

Value relates to the ValueSelling Principle: *People Make Emotional Buying Decisions for Logical Reasons.* After all, if the business and personal values of making the purchase are not firmly entrenched in the prospect's mind, he is not likely to be motivated to make the purchase.

ValuePrompter
Remember that it is not your job to create value; rather, you must uncover what is valued and connect your solution to it.

Should I Buy relates to the ValueSelling Principle: *People Need a Reason to Change.* Without a business issue, or the root cause of an underlying issue to solve as well as a personal issue to address, the prospect will not be motivated to continue a dialogue with you. At the same time, by establishing the root cause, and identifying how your product or service will uniquely solve their problems, you've connected the ValueSelling Principle: *The Product is in the Mind of the Buyer.*

Can I Buy relates to the ValueSelling Principle: *You Can't Sell to Someone Who Can't Buy.* If your prospect cannot make the final purchase decision, the sale will stall. If they are not the ultimate decision-maker, all is not lost. You can negotiate using your understanding of their personal issues for access to power.

Will I Buy relates to the ValueSelling Principle: *The Correct Use of Power Is Key.* You must establish a rapport with the prospect in their language so that they identify the true value of your product or service, and ultimately place their trust in you as a consultant who can help to solve their business and personal issues.

It is important to note that qualifying your prospect is not a one-time event, nor is it a checklist of activities; it is fluid. Your prospects do not operate in a static world. Situations change — people change jobs and budgets are cut — and even the most qualified prospects can quickly become unqualified. As you will see, qualifying your prospect is powerful not only when initially identifying your prospects, but for re-qualifying them when the sales cycle stalls.

Once you are able to satisfy each component of the equation: *Can I Buy, Should I Buy, Will I Buy* and *Do I See the Value,* you can map your sales process to the customer's buying process and develop a plan to prove that you can and will do all that's presented in your sales pitch.

Here are the concepts you can apply today to eliminate sales efforts that result in No Decision:

- Connect the Dots in Their Language — Determine what drives them by getting them to define their business and personal issues.

- Confirm and Confirm Again — Get the prospect to define their unresolved business issues and the unique solution it will take to resolve them, as well as their perception of the value of being able to resolve their business issues.

- Should They Buy — Identify the root cause of the problem that you need to solve.

- Can They Buy — Determine whether your prospect has the ability and authority to purchase.

- Are They Willing to Act — Uncover the prospect's true willingness to enact a change and confirm their perception of the company's willingness to do the same.

- Reconfirm the Value — Does the prospect perceive enough business and personal value to move forward with your solution?

CHAPTER 4:
Asking the Right Questions

"You have two ears and one mouth so that we can listen twice as much as we speak."
    Epictetus, Greek philosopher (A.D. 55-C.E. 135)

Salespeople have historically been stereotyped as self-serving and untrustworthy because they are perceived to be only pushing their products and services, not listening and providing creative solutions. To overcome this history you must evolve as a business consultant. As sales professionals we are all in the customer success business, not merely the selling profession. Asking the right questions at the right times and actively listening to the answers is the fuel of the ValueSelling process. Understanding the flow, structure and organization of the questioning is the repeatable aspect of the process.

Most salespeople believe they can explain and tell someone everything they need to know about their product/service. Based on their command of language and eloquence in presentation, the prospect will be convinced and compelled to act. But selling isn't merely telling. Our clients aren't looking for people to talk at them. They are seeking people interested in them, in their perspective, and who care enough to listen.

Sales is not about telling, it's about managing conversations so that the customer comes to the same conclusions that we have come to with first-hand knowledge and experience. At the highest level, ValueSelling is about conducting better conversations with our customers and prospects that are targeted, helping each of them through their purchasing decisions and creating long-term customer relationships.

The most successful salespeople I know are also the most curious. They are truly interested in learning about the companies and individuals they work with. They aren't interrogating them. They are conversing with them and managing the conversation to learn the critical things they need to know to be successful in helping their prospects. They realize what many of us struggle to understand: We often demonstrate more value to our customers through the questions we ask than the answers we give.

A good friend of mine, also Senior Vice President of a Fortune 25 Healthcare company, and a long-time ValueSelling advocate once related this story: As a sales representative for the company offering the latest advances in healthcare technology back in the late 1990s, he was struggling to make his numbers. He was in the bottom 30 percent of the sales force. The company's sales methodology focused on demonstrating ROI in terms of the financial justification of the processes used to serve the prospect's customers quality of life issues.

When the company adopted the ValueSelling methodology, a light went off for him.

When I finally internalized the idea of asking the right value questions, he realized his interactions with customers and prospects had similarities to a rollercoaster ride.

"To me, ValueSelling is like the protective mechanism built on the first hill of a major roller coaster ride," he said. "Shortly after leaving the boarding station, cars carrying passengers engage a chain that pulls them up to the top of the first big hill, which provides the momentum needed to carry the cars and passengers throughout the ride. As you ascend that first hill, you hear the 'clank, clank, clank' of the safety device built in to protect riders from rolling back in the event that the chain fails."

He began to think of himself as the chain pulling his customers up the hill; ValueSelling was his safety mechanism to ensure that he carried his customers up over the top. In both cases, the roller coaster ride and the sales process, each has a safety mechanism to protect against failure. If the chain breaks on the roller coaster, you only slide backward to the point of the last clank — maybe a foot or two. Similarly, when executed correctly, ValueSelling is the mechanism that keeps sales people from going back to the start of the sales process in the event that the process stalls or the customer gets cold feet.

By asking the right questions and gaining agreement each step of the way, he was able to retrace the issues and the agreements they'd made in order to keep his customer moving up the hill to agreement.

For him, the questioning process reignited his sales efforts. Within a year, he was the company's number one salesperson and a member of the 100 Percent Club — meaning he met his sales quota every quarter. He was voted Rookie of the Year as well, and winner of the company's Sales Leadership award for replacing a key competitive installation.

I recently worked with the Vice President of Sales for a business services company. He had a big problem. The company had recently merged with a consulting company. As part of the integration, the sales organization was expected to sell the traditional products and services, along with the new portfolio of consulting services.

Nine months post-merger, revenue from consulting was less than 2 percent of the total revenue and significantly under the expected revenue the merger was supposed to generate. The Vice President of Sales had a very short window to create a plan and execute it to rapidly grow the consulting revenue. The salespeople had been trained on the new products — yet the pipelines were not growing and the orders weren't coming in!

The traditional approach to growing a sales force to be proficient at selling across the complete solution portfolio has been to provide one high-powered, fast-paced presentation covering all the features and benefits. You've probably sat through a few of these meetings and product presentations yourself. And while you probably learned what the products and services do, you probably did not learn how to apply that knowledge to why your prospects would want or need those capabilities.

In my role as consultant to the Vice President, I suggested that the sales force include a conversation about their prospect's business issues in each sales call to identify any problems that could be solved with the company's professional services. They did this by asking their prospects and customers questions such as:

> "Are you having trouble finding skilled people?"

> "Are recent layoffs making it difficult to get projects completed?"

> "Do you have trouble focusing on core responsibilities because non-essential tasks are taking up your time?"

By incorporating those simple questions, the company's consulting sales jumped to $100 million the very next year.

What made the difference? Rather than focusing on the features and benefits of their solutions, the salespeople instead focused on the needs of the prospects. Some of those needs may not have even been recognized at the time the question was asked — but they were surfaced and acknowledged as a result of the questions asked.

Like most sales professionals, you are probably highly knowledgeable about the capabilities of the products and services you represent. That is a given. And you most likely have passion and conviction about them, and are excited about discussing those capabilities and their impact. However, being a "solution expert" alone is not enough; ultimately you end up trying to push products and services without really knowing whether or not your prospects actually have a need for them.

The difference lies in how you manage the conversation about those capabilities with your prospect. This is the skill side of sales and relationship-building, and the real crux of your ability to succeed. By asking "Who cares?" or "So what?" about every feature of every product and service you represent, you begin to understand why your prospects might care about how your products and services can affect their businesses. And rather than engaging your prospects in a discussion of why they need to buy more from you, you instead discuss what problems they need to solve. Once a prospect agrees that any such problem exists, it's an invitation to ask about their view of potential solutions — and to create a need for yours.

The better you are at understanding what business issues and problems your prospects are experiencing, the better you become at uncovering needs that your products and services can address, and the better you'll be at integrating your solution(s) into the context of your prospects' businesses. That's what being a "problem expert" rather than a "solution expert" is all about. Using this approach, you become more consultative in your sales process, and ultimately move beyond the role of vendor to the role of business advisor.

So how do you go about finding out the answers to those questions?

Quite simply, you begin by asking the right questions.

Asking is not just about getting your questions into the conversation. It's also about listening to the answers and directing the conversation. By actively listening and building upon each question to clarify, you demonstrate to your prospect that you are consciously competent. If you're simply waiting to ask the next question, you're not listening and you may miss critical information that the customer is willing to share with you that could affect your ability to make the sale.

Understanding how to ask the right questions is important, and it is the execution that is critical. It is not an interrogation. It is a conversation, or series of conversations. It's all part of building relationships and gathering the information needed to help your prospects understand that your offerings are the best solution to address their business challenges. The execution must be conversational and natural.

There are three types of questions we want to ask at every phase of the prospect qualification process:

- Open-Ended

- Probing

- Confirming

The Open-Probe-Confirm Process will contribute to your rapport and deepen the relationship you are developing each prospect. Your interpersonal skills and rapport are critical here.

ValuePrompter
How you ask is equally important as what you ask.

We ask certain questions at certain times for specific reasons. It paints the landscape for us to describe, demonstrate, and deliver our capabilities, differentiators, and business models in a way that will enable us to be successful, gain their trust, and win the sale. The questioning process also gives us a process to back up the customer in their buying cycle when things go wrong or change. For most of us, these interactions happen both in real-time and over time.

Executing and managing the Open-Probe-Confirm Process is the key to sales success. If you're ever stuck in the sales process, you can use these questions to go back and reconfirm or re-qualify.

The Open-Probe-Confirm Process

Asking open-ended questions is the way to get your prospects to open up and share information about their businesses and what's important to them. There is no right or wrong answer — it is exposing their view. This helps you understand your prospects' situations and the context within which they are operating. Good probing questions also direct and expand your prospects' perspectives, getting them to think about issues they might not yet have considered. This is the stage in the sales process where we do our investigative work to get at the root cause of the problems and issues facing the organization along with their perspective.

The sequence of these questions is important:

STAGE 1 — Open-Ended Questions

The purpose of open-ended questions is to learn the prospect's perspective. When qualifying a prospect, you are going to ask an open-ended question to initiate a discussion of each area: Their view of business issues, problems, solutions, value, who makes the decision, and what will you need to do to be convinced. It establishes our credibility and interest in them — because we are asking them first, before we begin positioning and explaining. Open-ended questions are our vehicle to learn what the customer thinks at any given time. It is the springboard for the whole conversation. Naturally we tend to open conversations with open-ended questions: "Tell me about your day," or "Can you explain how this works for you now?" They are a natural way to get the conversation going. This is simple — not complicated!

Open-ended questions do not have a yes, no or "right" answer. They demonstrate that you are seeking to understand your prospect's world and perspective, especially on an initial call. Using open-ended questions, you might find out what they may have done to try to resolve certain business issues in the past, or uncover what prospects think they need to overcome certain problems.

Sample open-ended questions:

"Can you explain why..."

"Would you tell me more about..."

"How would you describe the problems related to ..."

When you get onto a topic that you need more information about, you next move to probing questions.

STAGE 2 — Probing Questions

Here is where you dig deep into details. For example, if your goal is to learn more about the company's profitability and the components which may put their profitability at risk, you would begin probing for typical barriers to profitability.

Probing questions seek to uncover more specific conditions based on the information first gathered using open-ended questions. Probing questions are closed questions; they will have a yes or no answer. And keep in mind that you may need to ask quite a few probing questions before you get to a couple of yeses. They also establish your credibility by revealing your knowledge of the company, industry or problem and solution, and further underscore your desire to understand. Probing with purpose can help you uncover specific areas — recognized or unrecognized by your prospect — which further demonstrates your ability as a problem expert.

Sample probing questions:

"Is it because..." (Business issue and problem probe)

"Do you find..." (Business issue and problem probe)

"What if you could … " (Solution probe)

"Have you ever experienced difficulty with..." (Problem probe)

If you are selling a product or service that isn't well-known, it's more important than ever that you get a handle on their perspective of solution because they may have an unrealistic expectation or have an issue that can't be solved.

STAGE 3 — Confirming Questions

Asking confirming questions is simply to confirm that we understand and gives them opportunity to clarify and deepen our understanding. If we have been dialoguing over a period of time sometimes the situation or their view has changed.

The art in confirming questions is to use reflective listening — confirming and playing back the actual words the customer has used and affording them the opportunity to elaborate. Don't assume meaning. Ask for understanding.

The key isn't the wording, it's the content of the question: "Have I captured the words and the language so that the customer and I are on the same page?", "Let me take a moment to ensure that I fully understand before we move on," or "Is there anything that you would add to that?"

Confirming questions seek to play back what the prospect has told you. This allows you to verify that what you uncovered with open-ended and probing questions is correct and current. They demonstrate to our prospects that you understand their paradigms, and help to verify that their perspectives have not changed as you move through the course of the sales cycle. Confirming questions not only demonstrate that you have listened; they can also serve as trial closes and checkpoints throughout the process.

Sample confirming questions:

"So, what you're saying is ..."

"Is it correct to say that ..."

"Did I hear that ..."

Once you discover a situation that's different from your understanding, go back to the two types of questions. Ask an open-ended question and begin to probe to deepen your understanding and raise the conditions you need to raise. Regardless, you must listen for the answer in confirming so that your response, or next question, is logical to the conversation.

As discussed earlier, ValueSelling directly links your prospect's top business objectives and issues with your products and services as a means to achieve those objectives by resolving those business issues. The ValueSelling Process and prospect qualification progresses through four phases:

1. Learn about your prospect's business issues.

2. Uncover problems and connect our solutions to solve problems, thereby resolving those business issues. (We call this creating a Differentiated VisionMatch.)

3. After confirming a Differentiated VisionMatch, develop the value of that VisionMatch with the power person.

4. Create a Plan to justify moving forward with a business relationship.

Mastering this Open-Probe-Confirm Process is fundamental to developing trust and rapport with your prospects. The key to your success lies in your ability to listen and understand what the prospect tells you, and to integrate what you learn from them into the ValueSelling Process.

How do you turn it around when you're not getting the relevant information?

When you're dealing with a prospect who is aloof or distant, he may have a competitive alternative in mind and may not be willing to give you information. While managing the questioning process, and asking consciously competent questions that display your understanding of the issues, look closely for the reaction from that person. If you are getting resistance, you may want to ask why. Do they not acknowledge their issues and problems? Do they have a view of the solution that doesn't include you? If so, asking open-ended questions will give them the opportunity to tell you that. The first principle of ValueSelling is that *People Need a Reason to Change.* They also need a reason to meet with us and participate in the conversations.

Here are the concepts you can apply today to manage your conversations and successfully navigate the sales process:

- Be Curious — You demonstrate more value to your customers through the questions you ask than the answers you give.

- It's Not About You — Focus on the needs of the prospects first so that you can differentiate your features.

- Be a Solutions Expert — The better you understand your prospect's business issues and problems, the better you can uncover needs that your products and services can address.

- Simply Asking is Not Enough — To gain a clear, complete understanding of your prospect's needs, you must ask the right questions in the right order:

  - Open-Ended Questions enable you to learn the prospect's perspective.

  - Probing allows you to uncover specific details.

  - Confirming enables you to clarify for understanding.

CHAPTER 5:
Crafting the Differentiated VisionMatch

"If you want to make good use of your time, you've got to know what's most important and then give it all you've got."
                    Lee Iacocca, Business Executive (1924-Present)

Our prospects always have alternatives — with competitors and with the status quo. The only way for you to consistently lock out those alternatives in the mind of the prospect is to uncover and create need for the uniqueness you bring to the table. It is critical for you to have the skill to not only understand and articulate how and why your product or solution is different, but to answer the questions, "Is it worth it?" or "Does this matter?" from the prospect's perspective.

META Group Inc., an information technology research and technology firm, was founded in 1998 by two former Gartner Inc. executives. Their goal was to develop a better research-based business than that of their competitors, Forrester Research and Gartner. By 2003, the company was in its third straight year of operating at a loss. John Daut joined the company as Vice President of Sales in August of 2003.

The research business was struggling as a whole because of declining budgets and greater competition, but META Group was foundering more than any of its competitors. John's first task was to conduct an autopsy of their sales process and diagnose what could be done to turn their financial situation around. He determined that "the tail was wagging the dog."

"There was no quality control, and no conscious understanding of what value the clients associated with our business," John told me. "If we won a client, the sales reps assumed that it was because the client liked them. If we lost, it was assumed that price was the cause. There was no understanding of why we won or lost business."

John had been trained in ValueSelling in a previous position and was comfortable selling his executives on incorporating the methodology. "We needed a common language and process that would take us from point A, learning what the client's business issues were, to point B, communicating why our services were clearly the best for solving those issues."

"ValueSelling helped the salespeople understand the sale as a by-product of addressing the business issue. Before ValueSelling, they were aware that they needed to solve issues, but they didn't understand how to evaluate the difference between true value and unimportant issues."

Within a year, the company was winning 80 percent of the opportunities it pitched, and on April 1, 2005, Gartner, Inc. purchased the company. According to a statement released by Gartner on April 1, 2005, announcing the purchase:

> *"Today, we significantly increased the depth and breadth of our sales coverage in the vastly underserved market for IT research by welcoming more than 100 highly-trained salespeople from META — individuals who know the marketplace and our products. With the META acquisition now complete, Gartner is a stronger, more broadly based company than ever before, with increased capacity to reach new customers and the ability to provide current users of IT research and analysis with enhanced products and services."*

The acquisition was a testament to the work the team had done to become a world-class sales organization. Not only did they successfully differentiate their offering in a highly competitive environment; they also perfected their ability to manage the conversation with the prospect so that they could drill down to the business issues and create a mutual vision of what the prospect's world would look like after purchasing META Group's solutions.

We call this "Crafting the Differentiated VisionMatch", and it involves three components:

Step 1 — Uncovering the Business Issue

The business issue is the high-level barrier that a company faces in achieving the stated business objectives. It is typically top of mind for the entire organization and is often the key criteria executives are measured by and even compensated on.

Often, the business issue is overlooked by sales professionals. Many sales reps have become savvy at understanding their prospects' business objectives but lack the understanding of the issues that may make that objective difficult to reach. Since a fundamental principle of ValueSelling is "People need a reason to change," an understanding of the objectives may be incomplete if your prospect does not see any difficulty in achieving those business objectives; he or she may not have a reason to change or consider your products and services.

Step 2 — Develop the Problems

Once the business issue is identified and confirmed, it is important to uncover the problems or challenges that make that issue difficult to resolve. Depending on the products and services you offer, you will uncover with the prospect those problems which you understand are likely to be causal to the business issue.

Step 3 — Develop the Prospect's View of the Solution

The last step in crafting a Differentiated VisionMatch is identifying a solution that can be applied to overcome your prospect's problems and, therefore, resolve the business issue. As we showed earlier, a VisionMatch is confirmation that the buyer's business issue and problems can be resolved with a specific solution (preferably yours!). It is important to understand the prospect's view of what they think it will take to resolve their business issues and problems BEFORE providing a detailed sales presentation or pitch.

We want to uncover and raise the consciousness of our prospects to all of the problems we're capable of solving before we get into creating and discussing the solution with the customer. This is the key to locking out competitive alternatives.

You might have a variety of smaller competitors that sell pieces of what you can offer. They can only provide point solutions to a single problem or an incomplete set of problems. If you can uncover a multitude of problems that only you are capable of resolving in totality, then you are in a position to eliminate the competitive alternatives.

To craft a true Differentiated VisionMatch, you must include the prospect. The fact that the salesperson understands the components of business issues, problems and solutions and their connection is not relevant in a VisionMatch. The VisionMatch is a confirmation that the prospect views the three elements in the same way.

We begin with the end in mind. It is understood that as sales professionals we have a deep understanding of our capabilities, the reasons prospects and clients use our services, and the benefits we bring to both the businesses and individuals we serve. Our skill as a sales professional lies in our ability to manage the conversation to uncover the prospect's view of the world, surface conditions they may not yet have considered, and mutually create a solution that will enable our prospects to achieve their goals.

So start with your solution. Ask yourself: What do we provide that is different or unique from any alternatives? Once you understand that, ask yourself: Why would a company or individual need that capability?

You can now shape those statements into your probing questions in a way that will get your customer to understand and confirm, in their own terminology, how your product uniquely solves their business issues and problems and satisfies the questions they must resolve in order to purchase:

Should I Buy? Does the prospect have a burning issue that can only be resolved with the products and/or services that I offer?

Be aware, however, that your job is not to decide what you think your prospects' problems are and to tell them your solution; your job is to use the Open-Probe-Confirm Process to help them articulate what they think the problems are and what they think they need in order to overcome the problems.

ValuePrompter

If you lack trust and rapport, your prospect may resist developing a Differentiated VisionMatch and will likely ask you to just present your solution.

The diagram below shows where business issues, problems and solutions fit into the ValueSelling process. To be successful in any selling situation, you need to understand — and connect to — your prospects' business issues.

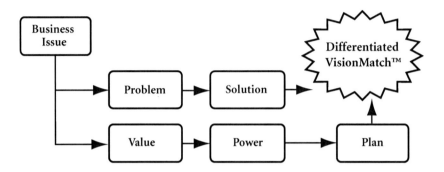

Uncovering Business Issues

Every organization has critical business issues that need to be addressed and resolved in order for certain business objectives to be achieved. Business issues are generally related to the overall objectives of increasing revenue, increasing profits, increasing market share and/or improving cash flow. By uncovering these issues, you will be able to identify how your product or solution can uniquely impact the success of the organization.

Examples of business issues include:

- Cost management (increasing profits, improving cash flow)

- Competitive challenges or losses (increasing market share)

- Time to market (increasing profits, increasing market share)

- Time to revenue (increasing revenue, increasing market share)

- Regulatory Issues (compliance such as Sarbanes-Oxley or HIPAA)

With each of these business issues come many problems, i.e., difficulties that prevent prospects from being able to satisfactorily address or resolve their business issues.

Examples of problems include:

- Additional or unnecessary steps (time to market, cost management)

- Lack of skill or training in new areas (competitive challenges)

- Difficulty securing personnel or resources (time to revenue)

- Changes in technical or regulatory support requirements (time to market)

- Mistakes common to manual processes (cost management)

- Redundant processes (cost management)

- Not understanding variable cost contributors (cost management)

- Managers approve discounts (time to revenue)

- Unit labor costs too high (cost management)

The key to solution or consultative selling is becoming the diagnostician guide for the prospect to uncover the root causes. In ValueSelling, it is critical to become the issue and problem diagnoser — before prescribing your solution. Think about the last time you went to your doctor. You may have been complaining about a headache or some other ailment. The doctor doesn't start by writing you a prescription — rather he begins by asking some basic probing questions: Has anything changed in your environment? What about your diet? He attempts to get at the root cause of your symptoms prior to offering a solution. ValueSelling sales professionals follow this same process.

So how can you uncover your prospect's business issues? You ask them. One of the most powerful and repeatable facets of ValueSelling is the questioning process.

The Ken Blanchard Companies is a global leader in providing sustainable, common sense leadership, team and organizational training and development solutions. In 2003, the company was looking to grow its revenues (business issue). While their successful sales representatives intuitively understood the need to sell the value of their offering, the majority of the sales team struggled with how to demonstrate that value to prospects (problem). They conducted a pilot of the ValueSelling Framework (solution) with a select group of sales leaders. Sarah Caverhill, East Coast Regional Director, helped to head up the effort. The pilot validated her belief that "if you can't get to the business conversation, you won't sell."

"The business conversation should be your starting point. A lot of people can get out there and ask, 'How is your stock today?', but they don't know how to ask the next question, or they believe that asking questions shows a lack of knowledge," Sarah explains. "In reality, it's an effective avenue to categorize what you know, and figure out what you don't know, but need to know. By incorporating the open/probe/confirm process, it forces you to delve into the root causes of the prospect's business issue. Collaborating with the client is far more effective and the relationship is tighter."

According to Stephen Covey, author of *The Seven Habits of Highly Effective People,* a paradigm is defined as a unique framework through which an individual views the world. It is formed through a person's education, experience, belief system and value system. In terms of the ValueSelling Framework, an important point to remember is that a Differentiated VisionMatch must include the prospect's paradigm.

Through the process of creating a Differentiated VisionMatch, you're letting the prospect see what his world will be like after he acquires your product or services.

As a sales professional, it is your responsibility to guide the prospect with your probing questions that incorporate solution-specific wording. Let's use ValueSelling as an example. Instead of opening the business conversation with, "One of things that makes ValueSelling great is that it helps you differentiate and sell the value of your solution," you want to begin the conversation with questions. The correct approach is to surface the problems you know you can address:

> "Tell me about your current sales and how it is working for you and your team? Do some of your customers have difficulty understanding the value of your solutions?"

> "Do you have to discount your solutions to win the business?"

> "Are you having difficulty reaching the ultimate decision-makers?"

> "Can your sales executives regularly forecast their business results accurately?"

By shaping questions that properly uncover problems we know we can uniquely solve, we begin to create the "hook" for our solution to rest upon and are more likely to become differentiated in their mind.

Differentiated or Just Different?

Differentiation is what sets you apart from the competition. It solidifies your product or service as being uniquely qualified to address business issues and problems in a way that the prospect may not have considered, experienced, or even thought possible. Differentiation positions you as a sole-solution provider to the problems that they have.

The first step in this process is to understand what is unique about your products, services and solutions. In order to do this effectively, you must become an expert in not only your products and services, but the competition's solutions as well. Often our competition is not just another solution provider with similar products and services — it could also be an internal solution or status quo.

A client of mine is a senior sales executive for the leading private aviation provider in the U.S. She is responsible for selling their private aviation services to high-net-worth individuals and corporations in the South. Interestingly enough, the company she works for is not only the biggest provider of these services, it is also the company that has a list price or hourly rate significantly higher than all other private aviation alternatives.

So I asked her why people paid more for her company than for less price-competitive alternatives. Her answer was very interesting.

Often her prospects contact her and they are basically shopping for price. The conversation starts something like this:

"I am interested in flying privately — what are your rates and what types of planes do you have?"

At this point, my friend has two choices. One, she could answer the question. Two, she could try to get a little more information from this prospect. She chooses the latter and always tries to get more information. Until she can create the context of what her "solution" is relative to the customer's needs, she will always be pigeon-holed as more expensive. So the questioning begins:

"Where do you fly? And how often?"

"Who is typically flying with you?"

"Is there ever a time where that changes?"

"Could you foresee a time when you would need to make arrangements on very short notice?"

Oftentimes, one of these questions will raise an area that is critically important to the prospect.

As she related this story to me, it occurred to me that the salesperson probably has an arsenal of questions, but she skillfully pinpoints the one problem that best fit that prospect's situation, and she can deliver the one and only product that can solve that problem.

Differentiation is the process that sets you apart from the competition in your prospect's mind. You could be different in twenty categories, but if your prospect cares about only one of those categories, then you really only have one "differentiator" that matters. Failure to differentiate from the competition will likely result in increased objections and more intense price negotiations.

A **Differentiated VisionMatch** is a confirmation with the prospect that your solution resolves your prospect's issues and problems better than any alternative. To craft a Differentiated VisionMatch, you need to uncover problems that you are uniquely qualified to address (and that they may not have thought of) and position yourself as the one and only solution partner.

ValuePrompter

Differentiation is the art of crafting need for the unique elements of your solution through specific probing questions.

To begin the process, determine which elements of your solution are unique or better than the alternatives. There are five primary areas upon which you can differentiate:

- Capabilities
- Terms and Conditions
- Convenience
- Risk Mitigation
- Price

"Capabilities" refers to the products you represent — their features, functions and deliverables — along with any related accessories and/or services. Generally speaking, this is where the largest degree of Differentiation comes in. Certainly, this is where most companies strive to teach in their product education.

If your products and services are somewhat commoditized, i.e., there is negligible difference between your products and your competitors', Differentiating on "terms and conditions" may be warranted. Examples include offering more favorable payment terms or longer warranties than your competition, or perhaps including a full money-back guarantee when your competition says all sales are final.

"Convenience" refers to how your products or services are delivered or whether your solutions are easy to implement. For instance, offering free training along with your automation system — as opposed to charging for it like your competitor — can be a powerful differentiator. In addition, many companies differentiate themselves as locally available to support their clients.

"Risk mitigation" refers to making a purchase less risky for the prospect by providing proof of your ability to deliver on your promises. Industry leaders often differentiate themselves in this way.

"Track record of success," or "financial fortitude for growth and future product enhancements," may be manifestations of this.

Years ago, there was a saying among information technology professionals: "Nobody ever got fired for buying IBM." IBM may not have always had the leading-edge technology, but their customers knew they'd be around to see the implementation through to the end — and beyond.

"Price" is the fallback differentiator that many of us want to avoid. After all, do you really want to be known as the low-cost provider? A sales professional who works for a small computer reseller in the Pacific Northwest told me that one of the first things he tells a new prospect is, "There is always someone willing to beat my price." This quickly establishes that his company is not the low-cost provider, and successfully weeds out those prospects solely looking for the lowest price tag.

Once you've decided where to differentiate, the next step is to determine what the prospect would have to articulate for that uniqueness to matter. In other words, probe with purpose to uncover what specific problem they would need to have in order for your solution to be relevant — and unique. If you don't uncover your prospects' need for what your products do differently, then your products are just different in a way that will not necessarily motivate them to purchase.

Keep in mind that savvy prospects will try to ignore your differentiation in an attempt to neutralize that difference and force the conversation back to price, making your job more challenging. The key is to not only know your own products inside and out, but to also be thoroughly knowledgeable about your competitors' offerings as well. After all, if you don't know what the competition's strengths and weaknesses are, you won't know what you are competing against, and you'll have no basis for identifying where your products are unique.

Here are the concepts you can apply today to eliminate the competition in the prospect's mind:

- Uncover the Business Issue — By understanding the business issues, you uncover the issues that may make the objective, or purchase, difficult to reach.

- Develop the Problems — By drilling down through each problem, you can uncover the challenges that make that issue difficult to resolve.

- Develop the Prospect's View of the Solution — Identify a solution that can be applied to overcome your prospect's problems and resolve the business issue.

- Become the Diagnostic Guide — Uncover the root cause of the problem or business issue for your prospect and you'll soon become a trusted consultant.

- Know Your Competition — The only way to successfully differentiate your products and services is by understanding the strengths and weaknesses of the competition.

- Key Areas of Differentiation — Capability, terms and conditions, convenience, risk mitigation and price.

CHAPTER 6:
Developing Value ... Both Business and Personal

"What is a cynic, a man who knows the price of everything and the value of nothing."

Oscar Wilde, Playwright, Novelist and Poet (1854-1900)

Many salespeople believe that they have a responsibility to tell their prospects the exact value that prospect will realize from their products or services. In ValueSelling, our process fundamentally disagrees with that premise. Value is customer-specific, and therefore while it is important to understand what is likely to accrue for a prospect, we don't actually create value for them. As sales professionals, we are going to uncover what each individual customer or prospect "values" and connect to that with our unique solutions.

Have you ever won a bid that you never, in your wildest dreams, thought you would win?

J. B. Bush, a ValueSelling associate, was once the president of a relational database software company that targeted law firms as customers. He was asked to participate in a bid situation by the chief information officer of a large New York City law practice. The request caught him off guard as this particular CIO had been the largest reference for a key competitor just the year before, and had purchased a smaller solution from another, smaller competitor the year before that. J.B. was hesitant to participate because he assumed that this CIO was simply conducting due diligence and had already made the decision to go with one of the other competitors. Although he didn't believe that his company would actually win the bid, J.B. was eventually coaxed into participating in the bid process. To his surprise, his company won the bid.

J.B. was perplexed as to why they won the business over competitors that the CIO had clearly favored in the past. "The installation went well, everything was running smoothly, so one day I asked this CIO why we got the business instead of our competitor," J.B. explains. The simple answer surprised him: "Well, J.B., in my first year we used the Access program. Last year I went with your competitor. Now I'm going with you because it looks good on my resume."

It was a lesson that J.B. would never forget. Never again would he neglect to ask about personal value, because it can and often does override business value in the mind of the buyer. Do you think any of your prospects have ever made a decision like this?

To be successful in any selling situation, you need to understand — and connect with — what is important to the person (or people) you are working with. The better you are able to help your prospects link the effect of your solution to their business and/or personal objectives, the higher the likelihood they will buy from you.

Value — perceived or real, personal or business — is the only thing that separates your products and services from the competition's products and services. It's a combination of tangible and intangible components that represent our prospects' perception — not our perception — of the impact a solution will have on their business issue as well as on their personal situation. In other words, they prioritize based on the value to the business — or business value — and often, the value to themselves personally — i.e., the personal value.

Business Value

Business value is customer-specific; that is, two organizations or individuals can make the exact same purchase for very different reasons — and often do so. For example, a sales director for a technology company was trying to sell a $100,000 inventory and pricing system to the number-one market leader in the wireless phone industry. It was going nowhere until he figured out how the system could be used to save them $1.7 million. He closed the deal within two days.

That same sales director was working with another company to sell a similar system. That company's procurement manager was not as interested in the cost savings as he was in how the system would affect the pricing department and whether or not training was included. When he learned that training was part of the package, and that the integration of the software was practically seamless, he bought.

As this example illustrates, you need to understand how your prospects will justify the purchasing decision from a business standpoint, i.e., the measure of value to the business. Those customer-specific metrics — whether tangible, intangible or both — need to be met to get approval or funding.

Depending on what you sell, value can be measured in either hard dollars or tangible return. It also can be measured in intangibles, often referred to in soft dollars. Both can be important. The interesting thing about intangible value is that the savings that results in this type of value typically cannot be measured in a single line item on in income statement or balance sheet.

The following table lists a few samples of potential business value metrics:

Hard Dollars (tangibles)

Output	Costs
Size of Order	Unit Cost
Number of Orders	Overhead Cost
Time	Quality
Downtime	Rejects
Overtime	Error Rate

Soft Dollars (intangibles)

Work Habits	Work Climate
Absenteeism	Employee Satisfaction
Tardiness	Commitment
Customer Service	Development
Loyalty	# Promotions
Satisfaction Rates	Successful Projects

Again, these are just examples; you need to understand your prospect's specific metrics and the likely impact your solution will have. As you develop ROI models and value propositions, keep in mind the ValueSelling Principle: *People Make Emotional Decisions for Logical Reasons.* Value has to be relevant to the prospect's business, and he needs to "own" it to believe it. Additionally, your solution has to connect to some form of personal value before the prospect will even consider it.

Personal Value

You know those MasterCard® commercials where the cost of, say, tickets to the ballet is one cost, dinner at a fine restaurant another, and "the look on her face: priceless"? Personal value is that priceless item.

Personal Value relates to the notion of "What's In It For Me" (or WIIFM). Even in a business setting, people's personal agendas and motivations will drive their behavior. Everyone is motivated. As salespeople, we want to understand what each individual's motivation is and try to connect to it. This is especially true for individuals who are managed by objectives and rewarded, recognized or compensated based on how well they meet those objectives. Either way, every executive has something personal to gain from solving a top business issue. Examples of this personal value could include: A promotion, bonus, recognition, increased credibility or being perceived as the good guy, a pioneer, doing the right thing or making a difference. Or as in the example before, building a resume or learning a new skill could provide enough value for anyone to make a purchase.

Here's a real-life example of personal value at work: A medical equipment manufacturer was working with a suburban hospital to sell surgical technology. The salesperson — we'll call him Bob — was working with a purchasing agent who had been with the hospital for ten years. Bob showed the head of hospital administration a number of ROI cost-saving charts in the hopes of convincing her to buy from him.

The executive accepted the charts, but was more interested in whether or not the equipment represented the very latest technology. As she explained it, "Our hospital has a strong reputation for having the best-trained doctors, the latest equipment, and state-of-the-art facilities. I need to make sure these doctors have the most technologically advanced tools to work with. My own reputation is riding on it."

If you don't know what personal stake your prospect has in the procurement decision, you won't have all the information you need to demonstrate the value of your solution and motivate your prospect to act. When personal value is high, your prospect will work with you to craft and articulate the business value, but if personal value is low, there is a good chance you will never win the business. Again, the challenge is to help your prospects see the value from their perspective, not yours.

ValuePrompter

At the end of the day, the only thing that matters is whether the customer thinks it's worth it. If they don't, they won't buy.

The following are examples of personal value:

- Monetary — Will they get a raise or bonus for solving the business issue?

- Status — Will they be recognized within their organization for their efforts?

- Self-Perception — Is the prospect insecure about their ability to solve the business issue?

- Security — Is the prospect at risk of losing his or her job if the business issue is not solved?

- Other — Has the prospect made mistakes in the past that they need to overcome to prove their worth to the organization? Are they in competition with another employee to find the best solution?

In the ValueSelling Framework, there are two prerequisites to beginning a value dialogue with a prospect:

The creation of a Differentiated VisionMatch must have already enabled the prospect to envision solving problems and thereby resolving a key business issue with your solution. If a Differentiated VisionMatch has not been fully developed, it will be impossible to articulate business value, because it accrues to resolving business issues. Only after a Differentiated VisionMatch has been created and confirmed can you begin to uncover the value of that VisionMatch.

You must have developed a high degree of trust and rapport. Prospects don't often have value discussions — especially as they relate to personal value — until they have a solid foundation of trust with the salesperson.

But how do you find out what's valuable to your prospects? Once again, you ASK.

In previous chapters, we described how to employ the Open-Probe-Confirm Process to qualify your prospect and manage the conversation. The same questioning process gives you the power of a structured dialogue that enables your prospect to visualize the connection between your solutions and the value to the business AND the value to them personally for being the one to bring the best solution to the table.

Asking questions often makes salespeople uncomfortable because they feel that they are inappropriately delving into a prospect's personal life. There is a subtle difference between asking what drives an individual and probing for insecurities. Interestingly enough, the higher you are calling in an organization, the more likely the alignment between personal issues and business issues becomes.

Often, executive compensation and bonus criteria are public information. For example, if you're dealing with the CEO (especially in a public company) each decision they make is a reflection of their performance.

It's imperative to understand expectations before you can meet objectives. But before you get there, you must have established trust and rapport to get to the personal issues. And remember, confidentiality is key — you must be trustworthy and credible — never use the information you receive about personal value in a public forum or in writing.

Stage 1 — Open-Ended Questions

Uncover the prospect's perception of personal and business value by asking Open-Ended Questions. Since value is customer-specific, we are going to want to understand their view of how this type of a solution would be measured. What would be the effect of resolving this business issue to your organization?

Stage 2 — Probing Questions

Use probing questions to pinpoint specific values that we can bring to the table and to further motivate your prospects to act. You can formulate value probes by looking at the prospect's original problems and then appealing to both his business and personal interests. If you have a solid understanding of the typical value your solutions bring to your prospects, you can turn those into probing questions. What would be the effect of improving the quality of your materials? How will you know that you are successful in this initiative? Remember that you must have already established a good rapport to obtain good insight to personal value and actually have someone tell you their thoughts.

Stage 3 — Confirming Questions

Verify that the value is compelling enough for them to do business with you by using confirming questions. You seek to play back what the prospect has told you so that you can verify that what you uncovered with open-ended and probing questions is correct. Confirming questions not only demonstrate that you have listened and that you understand; you can also use a value-confirming question as a type of "trial close." Once your prospect has articulated the value they expect to realize from your solution, resolving their business issue, you can confirm with a question such as, "if you were convinced that you could achieve that result, would that be enough value to motivate you to move forward with this purchase?"

Business Value	Personal Value
Open	
How would you quantify the impact?	How does this affect you?
What would be the impact on the business?	Does this have any bearing on you personally?
Have you thought about how big these Issues are?	Could this impact anyone personally?
Probe	
Can you quantify problem #1, #2, #3 ... ?	Would this have a significant impact on your career?
Can we estimate how much is being lost by not taking action on ... ?	Is this causing you any frustration, irritation, etc.?
Confirm	
Are there any initiatives with more value?	Is there anything more important to you?
Is this enough value to take action?	Where does this sit on your priority list?

Business Value Accrues to Resolving Business Issues

Value is directly linked to resolving our prospects' business issues, not by solving individual problems. Your goal is to connect to what the prospect values with the impact of your solution. Anything short of revealing the connection between value and the business issue means you are expecting your prospects to make this link on their own. It is for this exact reason that the business issue becomes a critical component of crafting a Differentiated VisionMatch. Business value accrues to resolving business issues. In other words, any product or service is void of value until it is applied to a business issue. There is no business value in solving problems that don't resolve the business issues.

Connecting to your prospect's view of business and personal value can be the missing ingredient in a successful sales cycle; the better you are able to help your prospects link the value of your solution to their business and personal objectives, the stronger the buy-in and therefore the motivation to take action.

On the other hand, if you and your prospect are struggling to articulate the business value of your offering, there is a very good chance that you don't have a business issue in focus. Moreover, if you are unable to connect to the prospect's personal value, you may be at risk of losing the sale altogether. You can often win when you have personal value without business value, but you will rarely win without some measure of personal value on your side.

Here are the concepts you can immediately apply to develop value with your prospect:

- You Can't Create Value — You can uncover what your prospect "values" and connect to that with your unique solution.

- Never Minimize Personal Value — What's in it for me is a motivator that will drive your prospect's behavior.

- Before You Discuss Value — 1) You must create a Differentiated VisionMatch that enables the prospect to envision solving problems and resolving a key business issue with your solution and 2) You must establish a high degree of trust and rapport.

- Find Out What's Valuable — Employ the Open-Probe-Confirm Process to understand the prospect's expectations.

CHAPTER 7:
Identifying Power

"Motivation is the art of getting people to do what you want them to do because they want to do it."

>   *Dwight D. Eisenhower, 34th President of the United States (1890-1969)*

"Can they buy?" is a critical component of qualifying a prospect; in other words, confirming that all the work you're doing to craft a differentiated VisionMatch and connect to the value of resolving those business issues is with the individual who has the authority — or power — to act. After all, as sales professionals, we are implementing ValueSelling to mitigate our own risk of wasting time and energy on those prospects who will never buy from us. In the corporate world, there are many more people who can say no than yes. Our goal is to only accept the "no" if it comes from the person who could have said "yes."

The concept of selling to power is such a simple one. Yet experience has taught us that it is often overlooked or taken for granted by many sales professionals. We have learned that many salespeople fool themselves into believing that someone other than the one with power can sufficiently sell for them internally. Sometimes they are right; yet often they are not.

ValuePrompter

Salespeople are surprised at the end of a sales cycle to learn that the person that they have been working with and has told them they have the power to decide and act, in fact, does not.

Has this ever happened to you?

You've established a high level of trust and rapport with your prospect. You've identified a burning, critical business issue, along with several problems that you know your company can address better than anyone else. You not only have a VisionMatch with the prospect, you've got a Differentiated VisionMatch.

You've even taken it one step further: Your prospect has actually articulated the value — both to the business and to him personally — in resolving the business issue you've identified with your solution.

You've confidently forecasted the business to your sales manager, perhaps even daydreamed about what you'll be spending the commission on. You're all ready to go for the close, when the prospect says those seven dreaded words:

"I'll have to check with my boss."

You cringe … you thought your work was done and that you had confirmation from the individual who could actually execute a purchase. You were wrong. You weren't calling on the power person, yet. Unfortunately, hours of time and hundreds (or even thousands) of dollars are often wasted in trying to sell to someone who is not in a position to buy, but is willing to work with you.

It happens to the best of us, and in fact it is the number one issue all sales executives grapple with: How do I uncover who really has the purchasing power for this? How do I consistently get to the real power person? And once I have them, how do I get to go back in?

Marty Rowland of Foliage Software Systems illustrates precisely why you need to connect with the decision-maker:

> *"While at the Pyxis Corporation, I was aggressively working to get the Pharmacy Automation business from a well-known medical center in Boston. Unfortunately for me, the Center had hired a consulting firm that did not support the equipment I offered because they were aligned with one of my competitors. An RFP was scheduled to go out within a month.*
>
> *"By obtaining access to power early on in the process, and by working hard to dig into their business issues, I was able to get a look at the RFP before it was officially released. It was specifically crafted to help one of my competitors, and very clearly put my products and solutions out in left field. But again, because I had access to power, and had taken the time to understand their business issues better than many of the people who actually worked at the medical center, I was able to create a significant amount of doubt in the power person's mind that the solution that they were moving toward would solve all of their existing problems.*
>
> *"By creating anxiety and doubt in the decision-maker's mind, I was able to get the prospect to redraft its RFP to address all of their issues. In the end I obtained a multi-million dollar order from the medical center and they remain a satisfied customer of Pyxis."*

Over the years we have worked with our clients to uncover what happens when they don't win the business or what happens when the salespeople don't deliver on their forecasts. Power is often the missing ingredient.

There are times when you will get lucky and an internal champion sells to power for you; however, our goal as sales professionals is to be deliberate, consistent and predictable, not lucky. If your goal is to improve your win rate and minimize your risk of loss to the competition or to status quo, you must eventually work directly with the ultimate decision-maker in every selling situation.

In order to sell to power, you first must gain access to him or her.

There are many reasons why salespeople have difficulty connecting to power. In my experience, the most common reasons include:

- Fear that they'll be over their heads and unable to conduct a value-added conversation with an executive

- Fear that they will undermine their relationship with the gatekeeper by going around them

- The assumption that they are wasting the executive's time

Interestingly enough, many of us will work harder to avoid making a mistake or looking stupid, and that effort may work against us in approaching the senior executives in our prospects. Contrary to what many salespeople think, I find that the higher you go in an organization, the easier the conversation is. With functional managers, the conversations tend to be very technical or tactical. You may end up discussing a single capability, technical feature or deliverable at great length and detail. With a CEO, you're typically discussing business issues (productivity, fiscal results to the company) and value.

There are a number of traps you can fall into when trying to determine who has the power and how to reach him or her:

Titles can be misleading. For example, a director at Microsoft may have more responsibility than a vice president at the bank. You must look closely at the roles, responsibilities, and span of control.

Power doesn't necessarily mean the most "executive" title. For example, ValueSelling Associates is in the business of sales training. Power for the majority of our prospects is the Vice President of Sales; yet in a few cases, it is the operations manager of sales who determines which sales training to employ. The only way to learn the difference is to do your homework and ask the right questions.

Power may be elusive. Political power can determine who the ultimate decision-maker is. For example, a vice president of R&D and a vice president of Marketing may be fighting for funds from the same budget. You need to determine who of the two has the most influence and power to win the funds. Or cover your bets and do the work to craft a VisionMatch with both of them and tie it to their personal value.

Companies tend to be more risk-averse than in the past. This can manifest itself in who has the decision authority, as well as additional checks and balances within organizations. Research and experience tell us that more and more people at higher levels in the organization are involved in the buying process. In business-to-business sales, there are often as many as three to four additional people involved in even the smallest purchases, taking on a variety of roles:

Gatekeepers have veto power and may keep vendors and salespeople away from decision-makers. Some, like the administrative assistant who screens phone calls, are not buyers. If they are part of the buying team, they are the lowest-level buyers. At the same time, they are important as they may hold the key to access.

Economic Thinkers are responsible for getting the most from an organization's investment. They may do the negotiating and actual procurement, but they rarely use the product they are buying or care about its true value to the organization; the economic thinker's goal is to limit differentiation to price alone. Examples of typical titles of Economic Thinkers are: Buyer, Purchasing Agent and Contracting Officer.

Influencers are the additional people on the buying team who give recommendations but do not have final decision-making power. Influencers may have the clout to say no, but not the authority to say yes.

The *Power Person* is the ultimate decision-maker. It is the individual who has the most influence over the buying team in the final decision and has the authority to say yes. It is also the person who typically has the most to win or lose with your solution.

A *Sponsor* is someone who has been chartered with doing the evaluation or groundwork and is ultimately going to make a recommendation to power.

A *Coach* can be someone outside of the process or within the inner circle. They could be outside of the organization, but able to provide you with perspective and feedback on how you're doing.

Working with the various members of the buying team during the sales cycle is often required; certainly it can help you build sponsorship, credibility and trust. To effectively earn the buy-in of the team, you will need to employ the most powerful aspect of the ValueSelling process: Developing a VisionMatch with each team member so that you can connect to and confirm their individual perspectives. Work with each individual to understand their view of business issues, problems, solutions and value. Without this effort with the actual power person, you are not yet in a position to move forward, forecast the revenue, and close the deal.

ValuePrompter

Simply having an executive sponsor on board is not enough. To ensure success, you need to create a Differentiated VisionMatch and a strong connection to value, both personal and business, with the person who will make the ultimate buying decision.

Identifying Power

As sales professionals, we typically target among the highest levels in an organization those who we understand are typically the power we need to be successful. That said, we start in an organization wherever we can and then try to navigate to that ultimate decision-maker.

Once your foot is in the door, **"triangulation"** is a powerful tool for determining who has power. Triangulation is a method by which a salesperson relies on multiple sources to verify the truth. The reality is that you're asking the same questions of multiple people in order to ensure that your perspective is consistent and on target.

You can use triangulation to verify who holds the power in an organization by asking questions of the contacts you make at various levels of the organization. It's likely the responses you receive will vary; after all, different players in an organization have different perspectives as to who the decision-makers are. By asking multiple sources, you're more likely to discover the Power person's true identity. Guess what: We are going to use the same questioning process of open, probe and confirm to get a thorough understanding of power and our prospect's buying or procurement process.

Questions for uncovering the Power person:

"Who else besides yourself is involved in this decision?"

"How have decisions/purchases of this magnitude been made in the past?"

"Who else is affected by this decision?"

"Have you ever sought approval for this magnitude of a purchase before?"

"What or who could stop this purchase?"

"Once this decision is made, who needs to sign off on the paperwork?"

"Is there anyone who could veto your decision?"

"Who has the budget to fund this solution?"

"If you had to get more funding, who would you go to?"

Be careful not to ask questions that might threaten the trust and rapport you have developed with others on the buying team. They may not have the authority to say yes, but they may be able to say no — and might do just that if their confidence in you is diminished.

Accessing Power

After you have identified the power person, you may find that it's not always easy to gain access to that person. There are multiple strategies: Establishing Modus Operandi, Bargaining for Access and Campaigning.

Modus Operandi is a method for getting to power early in the selling cycle. The premise is that you dictate to the customer the conditions by which the sales process will unfold. One of the conditions — access to the senior executives or stakeholders in the prospect organization — is your standard "mode of operation." Without that access, there is no reason to continue to pursue the opportunity. It is a tactic that has often been used successfully by business consulting firms. During the very first meeting with a mid-level prospect, you set the expectation that you need to meet with the CFO, GM, CEO or other top executives or stakeholders that are most impacted by the success of the project or involved in the decision-making process.

How it might sound:

> "Our standard engagement mode includes an interview with all of the project's stakeholders early on in the process."

There are two caveats to this technique that you must keep in mind:

You must apply this tactic early and build the expectation right away. (After all, if you are fully engaged in the sales cycle, you probably will not be able to go back and say "Oh, by the way, I forgot to tell you that we need to talk to your executives before we go any further.")

You need to be firm with that requirement; in other words, be prepared to walk away if access you request is not granted. If you take this approach and your prospect does not agree to grant access, you can then disengage from the opportunity or attempt to bargain for access.

Bargaining for Access is another application of the ValueSelling Principle: *The correct use of Power is key.* In other words, you as a sales professional have power, too. Bargaining for Access entails identifying anything of value that the mid-level prospect requests during the sales engagement, and bartering for executive access in return. For instance, if your mid-level prospect requires an extensive demonstration or ROI analysis or anything else that would cost your company significant time, money or resources to execute, ask for time with a Power person in return.

How it might sound:

> "If I provide a comprehensive demonstration of all the facets of this system along with an ROI analysis, will you arrange a meeting for me with your CIO?"

Here are some examples of the bargaining chips you have the power to control:

- Information
- Expertise
- Reference contacts and/or visits
- Access to high-level executives at your company
- Loaner equipment, software or services
- Demos, trials, or embellished deliverables

Recently, I was contacted to speak at a national sales meeting by a meeting planner for the event. The contact had recently switched jobs, had worked for a client of ValueSelling and was familiar with ValueSelling. That prompted her to contact me. As it turned out, the sales meeting was going to be in San Diego — a plus for me, as that is where I live. Yet she was looking for a one-hour "keynote" presentation rather than a full training engagement. In speaking with her I quickly was able to craft a VisionMatch between my approach and their sales organization.

I was thrilled with the opportunity to speak at the sales meeting, yet I was concerned that without further clarification from the executives at her company, I might be at risk of falling short of their expectations. I tried to bargain for access to the COO of the company by trading sample presentation materials for the opportunity to share them with the COO and the meeting planner simultaneously. She agreed and arranged the meeting.

During the meeting that ensued I learned the COO's view of the issues, problems and solutions he needed for his sales organization. I was able to re-craft a VisionMatch for a one-day training workshop rather than a one-hour speaking engagement. In addition, the meeting planner felt like a hero for architecting a valuable resource for the sales and marketing team.

There are times when you don't have any access in an organization. Modus operandi and bargaining will not work. In those cases, you must create a plan to **Campaign for Access** within the company.

Campaigning is what most of us know as the true cold call. Writing, calling and messaging — either voice or e-mail — to get someone whom you have never met or maybe has never even heard of you to agree to an initial meeting.

One tactic to help with a campaign for a sales meeting or call is to turn the cold call into a warm call. Is there someone you know, work with today or have worked with in the past that can introduce you to your target buyer or target prospect? In today's world, where individuals are barraged by vendors and salespeople , if you can get an introduction, there is a significantly higher chance of getting that initial meeting.

Sometimes losing a sale can give you an opportunity to ask for references. Samantha Barrett-Wallis, of HRG North America — Events and Meetings Management in Toronto, was able to change her loss into a win: "After a proposal was turned down by a contact I've known for a few years, I asked her to come good on a previous promise to refer me to her counterparts at competing legal firms. Whether through guilt or the goodness of her heart, she provided me with marketing contacts in each firm — names, phone numbers and addresses — and gave me permission to use her name as a reference." I did and it worked — a number of those individuals are now clients of mine.

Assuring Continued Access to the Power Person

Once you've identified the power holder(s) and gained access to the executive suite, you might find yourself sent back into the organization's bowels for various reasons — perhaps to examine potential ROI, to craft a Differentiated VisionMatch or to work up a detailed Plan. When that happens, it is a good idea to negotiate a return ticket to that power person.

There are two different approaches you can take: Planned Access and Conditional Access.

Planned access involves asking for a scheduled meeting to ensure that you'll have continued access to the power person as the sales process moves forward. You might even consider scheduling status meetings or updates at regular intervals. Be sure to avoid closed questions that would elicit a yes or no response; that gives your mid-level prospect the opportunity to say no.

How it might sound:

> "After we meet with your team and consolidate our findings,
> I'd like to come back and share the results as they pertain to
> the business issue we discussed today. What is the process
> for scheduling that follow-up meeting?"

If you are not able to get a commitment for planned access,
conditional access may be an alternative strategy. In this instance,
you attempt to put some conditions around the circumstances
under which you may return. For example, you might ask for
return access to the power person in the event that an unexpected
problem requires a quick decision.

Anytime you are successfully able to pre-negotiate returned access,
you'll have a better chance of getting back into the executive suite.

How it might sound:

> "If the team survey uncovers some conflicting
> priorities, would it be okay to contact you directly
> to get your perspective on how to keep this initiative
> at the top of the list?"

Applying ValueSelling successfully is all about mitigating your risk
as a sales professional. That risk may be wasted time, no-decision
sales cycles or other nonproductive activities. Ensuring you
understand the power person's perspective is critical to mitigating
your risk. As sales professionals, we have to objectively understand
how our prospects are going to make decisions and leverage that in
our sales cycle. The key is to not fool yourself into thinking you're
working with the power person and forecasting the sale as a closure
when you're not.

Sarah Caverhill, of The Ken Blanchard Companies, encourages her sales team to find out what their prospects don't know and to use it as leverage.

> *"One of my sales executives had been trying to sell more into a long-term customer. She knew that she needed to move higher up in the company to sell more. She began by creating a VisionMatch for each of her contacts. By doing this, she learned that they didn't know the answers to the critical business drivers, or what the company was expecting from the investment. Fortunately, the people she worked with understood the value of answering the questions, and agreed to set up meetings with higher-ups. My rep was able to help her contacts increase their value within their organization by getting to the business issues they were hired to solve and by getting them into senior-level conversations, while moving further up the chain. The result was a sale of over a half a million dollars. Best of all, the client now truly looks to The Ken Blanchard Companies as a trusted advisor rather than a preferred supplier."*

Here are the concepts you can immediately apply to ensure that you connect with power:

- Avoid the Title Trap — A person's title is often a poor indicator of his span of responsibility. Clarify and confirm understanding by asking Open-Probe-Confirm Questions.

- Overcome Any Fears — The successful salesperson is the one who is prepared, regardless of their prospect's level in the organization.

- Embrace the Team — When working with purchase teams, be sure to develop a VisionMatch with each member to uncover their unique perspectives.

- When in Doubt, Triangulate — Use all of your sources to verify the truth.

- Employ Modus Operandi — Set the expectation that you need to meet with the CFO, GM, CEO or other top executives or stakeholders who are most impacted by the success of the project or involved in the decision-making process.

- Bargain for Access — To secure executive access, identify anything of value that the mid-level prospect requests in return.

- Maintain Contact with Power — Institute planned access or conditional access to ensure that the power person remains within your span of influence.

CHAPTER 8
Developing a Mutual Plan

"He who fails to plan, plans to fail."
Proverb

"So what will it take to get your business?"

At some point in your sales career, you've probably asked at least one prospect some variation of that question. Many sales professionals integrate this question into every potential sales engagement. The bigger question is: did you commit the answer to this question into a written confirmation with the prospect? And do you understand all the steps the prospect will need to complete to be convinced that you are the right alternative? In other words, did you send a follow-up letter or e-mail to your prospect confirming your understanding of the mutually-agreed-upon set of activities and milestones required for you to receive the purchase order, check or contract?

The **Plan** is a proof-of-concept agreement that demonstrates your understanding of what your prospect needs to be persuaded to do business with you. It outlines the activities required — by you AND by your prospect — to help you close the sale.

Here are a few activities that you might include in a mutual plan:

- Access all the right people, including the decision-makers

- Provide a demonstration of the solution or a comparison against a benchmark

• Verify all the details during a pre-proposal review so that you can close the business smoothly

• Start the legal and/or procurement or contracting process

It may be as simple as a letter or e-mail, or as complex as a pre-proposal document. The important thing to remember is: THE PLAN MUST BE MUTUAL. It must be created together with the prospect and documented to eliminate confusion and missed expectations. It is not your plan — it is a joint plan between you and the prospect.

Luke Papineau, a ValueSelling client, once explained to me how he successfully initiates a mutual plan:

> *"I work for a small reseller in the Pacific Northwest. We are constantly up against the big companies like CISCO, IBM and AT&T, yet I have always successfully differentiated myself and my company. One of the first things I always tell a new prospect is that there is always someone willing to beat my price. This quickly solves two issues: it tells the prospect that we do not offer the lowest price and tells me if the prospect is solely looking for price.*
>
> *"The customer deals I have won are solely based on the 'contract' I set up with them BEFORE I ever provide them with any answers. I use the analogy of a baseball game, where two teams come to the field at the beginning of the game and the umpire will state the rules of that particular game, so that BOTH parties are on the same page.*
>
> *"I offer the contract: 'prospect, you state that you have these issues (A,B, C, D) and it is costing you X number*

of dollars a year, and you have been trying to resolve this issue for the last six months and with no results. What happens if I can provide you with a solution that solves issues A, B, C, D that fits your budget needs and can solve it within a specific time frame?' If we reach an agreement then we proceed with the solution.

"By doing this, I have been successful in getting the prospect to share their business issues and problems, and I take this information and steer them to a solution to solving those issues in a manner that only our company can solve it in a manner that they need it to happen."

The plan is not your own personal to-do list that doesn't involve the prospect; rather, it is a written document to be crafted together by both you and your prospect. It begins with an understanding of the prospect's decision process, internal procurement processes and individual requirements to purchase your products and services. Every customer, whether an individual or a company, will make decisions uniquely. As sales professionals it is logical that we want to understand, leverage, and navigate that process with the prospect.

In the ValueSelling Framework, a well-developed plan benefits the salesperson as well as the prospect:

Benefit to You: Having a written plan allows you to stay in control of the sales cycle and avoid confusion regarding milestones and the initiation of a business relationship. The plan can also differentiate you from the competition in your prospect's mind. Not having a plan relinquishes control of the sales cycle to your prospect, and puts the sales professional in a situation where they can't predict what the result will be and when the prospect will buy.

Benefit to Prospect: A mutual plan specifies ways to prove that the solution you've presented is credible and reliable and demonstrates that you can do what you said you can do. This step will mitigate the perceived risk to the prospect of making a poor buying decision.

A key aspect of creating this mutual plan with your prospects is that it gives you the opportunity to bring them past their purchase and into realizing the value of your products and services. The plan is not over when you receive the order. It can include the activities that will contribute to a successful implementation for the prospect.

ValueSelling plans end when the prospect has achieved the value she expected and has resolved the business issue your solution was intended to resolve. This provides opportunities for you to "check in" with prospects from time to time to determine if there are other opportunities to help them with other business issues they may be struggling with. Resolving one business issue gives prospects a reason to do business with you in the future. It can serve to reassure the prospect that their decision is a good one; that they will be getting what they expect, and that it is focused on their business — not merely your order.

Jumpstarting a Stalled Sale

You've done everything right: Your prospect has clearly explained his business and personal issues, you've connected to those issues with a solution only you can provide, you are working directly with the power person, and you've agreed, in writing, to what you will do for the client. The only thing that you haven't been able to do is get them to sign on the dotted line.

ValueSelling associate J.B. Bush is an expert in helping his clients remove the roadblocks and jumpstart their sales. Here he shares an example:

> *"A client brought me in to strategize on a $2.2-million opportunity that had been forecasted to close six months previously, yet had slipped month after month.*

> *"To get to the root cause of the delay, I conducted an opportunity assessment with them. The sales team was able to confirm that their solution aligned to the business issue, it was clearly differentiated, and was committed to in writing and confirmed by the prospect. In other words, they had a Differentiated VisionMatch.*

> *"Next, I confirmed that they had uncovered the business value that would justify releasing the funds for the project. I also was convinced that the sales team understood the personal value of the key decision-makers. They clearly understood the decision-making process and had access to the key decision-makers. Their proposal was aligned and tailored to these individuals.*

> *"Last, but definitely not least, was the plan. What I discovered was an installation plan that outlined the activities from the day the purchase order was signed and ended on the "go live" date. Missing were the 12 months of activities that represented the efforts of both parties leading up to the purchase order. Additionally, the timing of when the prospect would actually realize the impact and financial benefits of the proposal was not included on this initial version of the Plan.*

"Having identified the gap, my client crafted a new plan that now included and summarized the 12 months of activities of both parties up to that point in the sales cycle. They also included the timing of when their prospect would begin resolving the identified business issues and when they would see the financial impact of my customers' solution. The last item on the plan was 'Mission Accomplished.'

"They presented the newly crafted, mutual plan to the prospect within two weeks of our meeting and had the signed purchase order seven days later."

Elements of the Plan

A written plan might take several forms; for example, a hard copy on your company's stationery or perhaps a simple e-mail to the prospect. To determine which format is best for your prospect, just ask them.

The plan should include a confirmation of the Differentiated VisionMatch (business issue, problems and solution) and value, as well as a call to action — either for you or for your prospect — to clearly indicate the next steps in the sales process. Below is an example of a formal letter. Determining the best way to craft this communication is part of the process.

Sample Plan Letter from ValueSelling:

[DATE]

Mr. Joseph Smith
Title
Any Company USA
123 Easy Street
Anytown, State Zip

Dear Joe,

Thank you again for your time today, and for the opportunity to discuss Any Company USA's sales organization. I understand you are in the process of evaluating sales training partners to assist you in the transition of the skill set and processes of your sales team.

The current situation, as a result of both your strategic and operational planning process, and the complexity of your sales environment, has increased. Your sales executives are transitioning from selling products to systems and that will require a new skill set that is consistent across the sales organization.

The top business issue is how to grow the opportunity size of each of your customers. Any Company USA prides itself in a great customer list and in providing a great customer experience. Revenue growth within that base is critical to reach the ongoing business objectives of the organization.

> *Reconfirm Business Issue and Problems*

Some of the challenges associated with achieving that objective include:
- Fighting off and differentiating against lower-priced competition
- Standardizing the sales team's skill set, which is "all over the map" from very tenured to less experienced
- Identifying the key decision-makers
- Uncovering the value proposition within the customer
- Motivating the customer or prospect to act

We also discussed that the ideal solution for Any Company USA will include:

> Reconfirm
> Solution

- A "ValueSelling" skill set and process
- Creating need for Any Company USA's unique differentiation and the differential value associated with that uniqueness
- Incorporation of relevant Six Sigma tools, processes and other relevant Any Company USA-specific sales tools
- Gaining and maintaining executive access
- Improved business acumen
- A framework for new product rollouts and applied product training
- A customized solution that is applicable and practical in your unique selling environment

The value to Any Company USA of a successful training rollout will be a systematic and organizational focus on the customer from the customer's point of view. The expected result is profitable revenue growth from within the current customer base.

> Reconfirm
> Business Value

The ValueSelling Framework™ by ValueSelling Associates is perfectly positioned to address your needs and enable your sales organization to meet and exceed its overall objectives.

At the core of ValueSelling will be the use of our unique ValueSelling Qualified Prospect Formula", which is a tool to develop the skills and process around the critical elements in a value added sales cycle. Our delivery methods are extremely flexible and we can customize our program to meet your specific objectives and incorporate your existing processes, tools, and best practices.

ValueSelling specializes in transitioning sales organizations from pushing product to selling business solutions. We enable sales executives to sell the full value of their products or services, thereby increasing their operating efficiency and enhancing their market leadership position. ValueSelling delivers a measurable impact to key sales operating metrics by identifying key initiatives and implementing the training, reinforcement, and measurements to insure success.

ValueSelling clients have experienced the following measurable impact by implementing the ValueSelling Framework:
- Reduction in discount rates
- Increased deal size due to up-selling and cross-selling
- Increased competitive wins
- Improved forecast accuracy

We will work with your organization to develop the specific metrics of where we will be able to track measurable impact.

The team to make the decision to partner with a sales training and consulting organization is being led by you and directed by Mike Jones.

> *Reconfirm Power*

You have shared with me your aggressive timeline for both selection and rollout. We are prepared to meet your timeline and work within your dates and deadlines. I have attached a timeline based on the dates and milestones as I understand them.

Sincerely,

Julie Thomas

President, CEO ValueSelling

****

Page 2

Any Company USA

ValueSelling Sales Transformation Timeline

Event	Date	Status
Initial Meeting: Joe Smith	2/9	Completed
Distribution of sales training RFP	2/14	Completed
Responses due by potential partners	2/21	Completed
Verify partner references		*

Pre-proposal review	2/22	
Selection of training partner	2/28	*
Announcement of ValueSelling approach and process	3/10	*
Customization and design of training program	*	*
Rollout of program to approximately 50 individuals	*	*
Reinforcement and ongoing process	*	*
Measurable impact realized within 90 days of training rollout	*	

You might have noticed an item called "Pre-Proposal Review" in the above list of activities. A pre-proposal review is a confirmation and presentation exercise that should be built into any Plan. It is a meeting with your prospect's buying committee, sponsors, influencers and power to review your findings and confirm that all of the information required to make a decision is in order. Reviewing this information reconfirms your understanding of the prospect's business and shows how you're able to address his challenges. It can also uncover any uncertainties in the prospect's mind, ultimately helping you address those issues and shorten your sales cycle.

During the pre-proposal review, you should determine whether your prospect is ready to do business and trial-close on an immediate timeline. If successful, you should be able to obtain your prospect's commitment to do business before you develop a final proposal.

The More Things Change

Imagine your prospect has told you that you'll get their business if you successfully demonstrate your product or service and provide a reference. You of course commit this agreement to writing and complete these proof steps, only to hear the prospect say that now she would like to try out the product or service for 30 days, "just to be sure."

Changes in the plan can be used as bargaining chips. If your plan is in writing and the steps in the plan have previously been agreed to by both you and your prospect, you'll have a stronger bargaining position. The best item to ask for in exchange for alterations to the plan is whatever will help close the sale faster.

ValuePrompter

If you do not have a written plan, or it is not formally confirmed in writing, then it will be difficult for you to bargain when changes occur.

How it might sound:

> "I understand your need to be confident in your decision. If I agree to provide the evaluation, will you then _____? (Any bargaining statement includes if … then statements. Fill in the blank with whatever you need to avoid further delays to the decision cycle.)

Here are the concepts you can immediately apply to ensure that you have established the rules of engagement that will ultimately lead you to a win:

• Before You Begin — You must have an understanding of the prospect's decision process, internal procurement processes and individual requirements to purchase your products and services.

• A Plan Is Not a To-Do List — A mutual plan outlines the activities required by you AND by your prospect to help you close the sale and mitigate the perceived risk to the prospect of making a poor buying decision.

• What You Include Protects You — Be sure to cover all the potential obstacles to winning the sale:

> Access all the right people, including the decision-makers

> Provide a demonstration of the solution or a comparison against a benchmark

> Verify all the details during a pre-proposal review so that you can close the business smoothly

• Start the legal and/or procurement or contracting process

• The Benefits Are Great — You maintain control of the sales cycle and avoid confusion regarding milestones and the initiation of a business relationship. Your prospect is convinced that the solution you've presented is credible, reliable and demonstrates that you can do what you said you can do.

• The Downside Is Greater — Without a mutually-agreed-upon plan, you risk the unknown. You may underestimate obstacles, such as the importance of key decision-makers.

• Use Plan Changes to Your Advantage — When your prospect requests a change in your mutual plan, request something in return.

CHAPTER 9:
Going for the Close

"Obstacles are those frightful things you see when you take your eyes off your goal."

> Henry Ford, American Industrialist, Auto
> Manufacturing Pioneer (1863-1947)

How many of these objections have you heard before?

"We really want to test your product in our environment."

"We need to extend the evaluation."

"Can we talk to someone who has been successful with this product first?"

"We need to set up another demo for … "

"I need to think it over a little more … "

How many of these objections have you heard before? You could probably add dozens more to include all of the objections and stalling tactics you've heard throughout your career. Not surprisingly, the more complex and the more costly your solution, the higher the probability of a delay in your ability to close.

A **Close** is defined as a decision by a prospect to do business with you. The decision is then followed with an action by the prospect, such as issuing a purchase order, signing a contract, remitting funds or any other written commitment to do business. It is the logical outcome of a well-executed sales process and results in paperwork.

By now you are very familiar with the four key components in the ValueSelling Framework. This is a good time to revisit your progress. To prepare for the close, these building blocks for success include:

Differentiated VisionMatch: You've established credibility by building a vision with your prospect that shows how your solution can address his problems and resolve her business issues better than any other solution. The prospect has confirmed the "linkage." To be differentiated, the prospect must also acknowledge that there is some element of your solution that is unique and/or different from competitive alternatives. (After all, you might be competing against more than simply companies like yours; maintaining the status quo or adopting an internal solution might be alternatives under consideration.)

Value: You've helped your prospect uncover the potential value — both to her and to the organization — accrued by resolving her problems and addressing the business issues, and answered the question, "Should they buy?"

Power: You've crafted the Differentiated VisionMatch and uncovered value at a level in the prospect company's organizational hierarchy where the authority to spend the money lies, thus answering the question, "Can they buy?"

Plan: You've validated with your prospect that your solution can be implemented with minimal risk to the organization as well as to the individual, and proven your capabilities are realistic and the value is attainable.

But what if you have NOT satisfied every part of the equation? Or what happens if something changes the situation and brings a once-qualified prospect out of qualified status? If there are any unanswered questions in the prospect's mind, or unclear linkages in any of the aforementioned elements, you will likely be met with an objection. An objection is a question, comment or doubt raised by the prospect that needs to be addressed before your prospect will move forward.

Overcoming Objections

Objections are questions or concerns that serve as barriers to closing the sale. Objections are different than reasons not to buy from you. Often, they are merely a request for more information or for clarified information by the prospect. They are a key indication that one of the four elements of the ValueSelling Framework has not been completely addressed from your prospect's perspective or that something has changed. Since our sales process is designed to make the prospect's buying process simpler, it is important to answer those questions and clarify the prospect's viewpoint. If the prospect has an objection, it must be on the table and addressed before you can move forward to the close. Unaddressed objections will block your sale every time, and you may not even fully understand why you were unable to close the deal.

So what do you do when confronted with an objection?

Most important, don't panic. It would be a far worse situation if your prospect did not raise the objection. By sharing the objection with you, the prospect has given you an opportunity to respond. Otherwise, you might lose the sale without ever knowing why you lost it.

Generally speaking, how the prospect asks a question or raises an objection provides clues into the unresolved subject and points you in the direction of where you have to revisit your sales process and do more work with the prospect.

Below are a few of the most common objections, along with suggestions for which aspects of the equation need strengthening.

"Your solution costs too much."

When cost is the objection, value is the answer every time.

A common belief in sales is that price concessions will motivate a prospect to buy. This could not be further from the truth. Discounting is not a cure-all to create urgency and close deals where a sales cycle has been incomplete. A great deal on a product or service that someone doesn't need or value probably isn't a great deal after all.

The first question to ask yourself and generally re-ask your prospect is whether the prospect confirmed that there was enough value in the solution to positively affect the business issue. Do they believe the value is attainable in their organization? The second question to ask is whether your prospect realizes or acknowledges the personal impact of moving forward with your solution. Assuming your price is fair, you don't have to be the low-cost alternative if you are truly differentiated. You have more work to do to uncover enough differentiated value to motivate action.

"I'll have to talk to my boss."

If you don't have a VisionMatch with the Power person, you are at risk that someone else, a competitor or competitive alternative, does.

Before you are ready to close, make sure you are calling on the right level and that the prospect has the authority to move forward. If you don't, re-craft your mutual plan with whomever you do have access to and bargain to meet with the ultimate decision-maker.

"I don't see the difference between your solution and the others we are reviewing."

Being different is not being Differentiated. As sales professionals, we must uncover the need for our differentiation using problem-probing questions. If your prospect does not agree that your solution is the best alternative for them, regardless of its unique capabilities, you need to work harder to differentiate your solution from the competitive alternatives. The key to creating a Differentiated VisionMatch is to uncover those prospect problems that only you and your solution can address.

"I am not sure that we are ready for this type of a product yet."

As your prospect gets closer to a decision, his fear of making a bad decision will increase. As sales professionals, one of our key responsibilities is to ensure that our prospect's risk is mitigated. Have you done what is necessary and required for this individual to be convinced? If not, he may not see a reason to move forward in the timeframe that you propose. Consider also whether this business issue is the most pressing challenge for the prospect. If you're attacking a secondary or tertiary issue, the prospect may be giving priority to an issue with a higher degree of urgency.

"I really need to think it over."

The "I'll think it over," objection doesn't pinpoint which part of the equation is missing. Your best bet in this case is to probe for further details:

"What is it exactly that you would like to think over?"

"Is there any clarification that I can assist with?"

"Has anything changed since we last discussed and confirmed your business issues, problems, view of the solution, etc.?"

Below is an example of how to deal with a prospect who wants to "think it over." Keep in mind that this level of questioning is dependent on your level of credibility and rapport with the prospect. You might need to make a judgment call as to how far you can pursue this kind of discussion.

Salesperson: Can I count on your commitment to do business with us?

Prospect: I'd like to think it over.

Salesperson: That's important. Many of our satisfied customers took the time to think over their decisions, and I'm sure you wouldn't spend the time unless you were seriously interested. Is that correct?

Prospect: Yes.

Salesperson: What is it that you want to think over? Is it whether we've addressed all of the problems you need to solve?

Prospect: No, you've been very thorough and you've demonstrated a good understanding of my challenges.

Salesperson: Is it whether we can enable you to solve these problems?

Prospect: No, your solution addresses all of our requirements. (There is a Differentiated VisionMatch.)

Salesperson: Well, is it whether we've been able to demonstrate enough value to motivate you to become a client?

Prospect: I guess I don't see value in acting immediately.

Salesperson: Can we go back and revisit the value of resolving these challenges sooner rather than later?

ValuePrompter
You will never close a sale when a prospect has an objection that has not been addressed.

Here are some additional tips for handling objections:

Clarify for understanding: Not all prospects ask exactly what they want to know. Before you begin responding to an objection, be sure you understand exactly what the objection is. Use confirming questions or rephrase the question.

ValuePrompter
Not addressing the true objection with your prospect increases the risk of losing the sale altogether. In other words, answering the wrong question with the right answer will not help you in the sales process.

For example, I have a client that is a consulting organization. They were working with a large East Coast-based hospital to sell and deliver their services. It was a competitive situation. When pulling together their final proposal, they had chosen to be extremely competitive and aggressive with their pricing and proposal. There was no "fluff" and no room for additional concessions or discounts.

After submitting the proposal, my client was called in to meet with the Chief Administrative Officer at this hospital. Once the meeting was underway, my client was asked about his pricing: how did they determine the prices, what was included, what was excluded, etc. My client became a little nervous, as he knew that if the hospital was seeking a lower investment level, he would be unable to accommodate.

He began to address the questions by asking another question first, clarifying what and why the pricing was in question. As it turned out, this prospect didn't think the price was too high. On the contrary, my client's proposal was actually the lowest one. The hospital was concerned that the pricing wasn't all-inclusive and that they would end up in a situation where the costs were not fixed.

By clarifying with questions he was now able to address the real objection, which wasn't price but deliverables.

Diagnose the Objection: Determine which area of the ValueSelling Formula is weak or underdeveloped. Here are some questions to ask yourself:

- Does your solution address a business issue that your prospect has acknowledged?

- Does the prospect agree that your solution would solve problems better than any alternatives, thereby resolving that Issue?

- Has enough value been quantified by your prospect to justify the investment in your solution?

- Does your prospect have the authority to make the purchase?

- Have you demonstrated your capabilities and proven your value to the prospect's satisfaction?

- Do you have a written plan for moving forward with a business relationship?

- Does that plan involve the prospect and include a specific date that will result in a business relationship?

Once you have clarified the objection and diagnosed which area of the Formula is affected, determine whether there is anything else that is keeping the prospect from moving forward. You want to surface ALL your prospect's concerns before you respond to any single objection. We call this the "Sharp-Angle Close".

How it might sound:

"If we can address and clarify the issue you have raised, how long before we can schedule delivery?"

Many salespeople come to us and ask for the magic words that will address their prospects' objections. Again, closing is the natural outcome of a well-executed sales process. Using the ValueSelling Process is the ingredient for success. Once you have diagnosed where the objection is coming from, you can then go back and confirm what you learned earlier in the sales cycle and reconfirm or probe for what has changed.

Negotiate to Win

Of course, given today's hyper-competitive markets, prospects are more risk-averse than ever. In any negotiating situation, your responsibility is to understand your prospect's criteria — as well as your own — and ethically create positive outcomes for all parties involved.

Negotiations should begin only after you have confirmed a Differentiated VisionMatch and established both business and personal value. Using the three key negotiable categories — Deliverables, Terms and Conditions and Pricing — with the following three strategies can help you navigate the rough sea of negotiation.

Strategy #1: Trade-offs

With trade-offs, your objective is to meet both parties' needs by trading items from one category with items from a second category.

How it might sound:

> "If you want this product shipped to multiple locations,
>   are you willing to accept different payment terms?"

Strategy #2: Embellishments

This strategy requires you to add incremental value in one category when you can't make a trade-off to accommodate the prospect. For instance, you may throw in deliverables that have little cost to you but are of large value to the prospect.

How it might sound:

> "If we expand the training class from fifteen to twenty
> people, are you willing to pay the same base price for
> each additional student?"

Strategy #3: Compromise
Compromise involves finding the middle ground in the same
category. Splitting the difference on price, payment terms or a
specific deliverable could be examples.

How it might sound:
> "If we can split the difference, can we move forward?"

When negotiating with prospects, there are a few points to remember:
First, be sure you understand the "need" behind your prospect's
position. Second, know your empowerment level; you could find
yourself in dangerous territory with either your company or prospect
if you commit to things that are outside of your span of control.
Third, maintain composure; respond rather than react and maintain
a high level of rapport every step of the way. Finally, know your
"walk-away" position; some deals are simply not worth what you
are being asked to give up.

Negotiating for success requires planning and strong communication
skills. Keeping the ultimate goal in mind — a positive outcome for
both parties — will increase your potential for successful outcomes.

Here are the concepts you can immediately apply to ensure that
you successfully overcome your prospect's objections:

- Don't Panic — If your prospect raises an objection, consider it
  an opportunity to clarify and reassure.

- Clarify for Clarity — Use the Open-Probe-Confirm Process to identify the root of your prospect's objection.

- Diagnose the Problem — Before you can address the objection, you need to understand which area of the ValueSelling Framework is lacking.

- Common Objections — What we hear most often, and how it relates to your process:

    "Your solution costs too much" — the value hasn't been clearly established.

    "I have to talk with my boss" — your prospect isn't the power person.

    "I don't see the difference between your solution and the others we are reviewing" — you haven't established a Differentiated VisionMatch.

    "I am not sure that we are ready for this type of a product yet." — You have not successfully mitigated the risk as it relates to their business issue or personal issue.

- Create a Positive Outcome — Once you've clearly diagnosed your prospect's motivation, use negotiation to increase their comfort level and mitigate their fear of risk.

CHAPTER 10:
Implementing ValueSelling

"Success is the maximum utilization of the ability that you have."
Zig Ziglar, Sales Pioneer and Motivational Speaker (1926-Present)

Now that you've learned the fundamentals of the ValueSelling Framework, and hopefully practiced the techniques by applying them to your selling situations, it's time to turn your newfound knowledge into action.

You've qualified a prospect using the Qualified Prospect Formula. You've identified and confirmed the business issue. You've confirmed the prospect's view of the problems that need to be resolved and the differentiation. You've established that there is enough value in resolving the problems from the prospect's perspective, and you've developed a plan with the power person. Heck, you've even managed to sell a few additional products or services that you've ignored in the past.

Congratulations — you have successfully used the ValueSelling Framework to turn your prospect into a bona fide customer!

Now that your customer has signed on the dotted line, what's your next step?

Customer Retention

Many salespeople are guilty of "hit-and-run" selling. They get the order and then disappear until the renewal is due or they want to upgrade that customer. The best salespeople retain their customers by staying in touch with everyone involved in the purchase decision throughout the life cycle of the relationship. From the end user to the decision-maker — they reinforce the buying decisions, uncover new needs and are accountable for deliverables and service.

If developed correctly, that plan you wrote with your new customer should not only prove your capabilities, but should also identify the anticipated results in terms of the value and impact of the solution. In other words, your list of activities did not end with receiving a check; rather, it took you and your customer through the implementation process — which you should monitor — and includes milestones where the value is actually achieved or realized — which you should confirm.

The business of "sales" isn't simply the acquisition of new customers; it is also the renewing and reselling of your existing customers. A top sales professional that I worked with once told me that he wasn't in sales; rather, he was in the customer success business. The sale of his product and service was a derivative result. A key aspect of your role as a salesperson is to maintain and grow the revenue from your existing customers. Losing customers is losing a key corporate asset. It typically costs a lot more to get a new customer than to keep one. Therefore, the most profitable business relationships are typically long-term in nature.

The concept of customer retention begins before the customer is won — during the sales process. People are satisfied when their needs are met and value is realized from their purchasing decisions. Reinforcing, communicating and reviewing the purchase decision throughout the relationship will help to solidify the business relationship over time.

Checking in from time to time, or at specific milestones of your plan, shows customers that you see them as more than just a series of big, fat commission checks. It also justifies the trust they put in you in the first place, which makes the buying process a lower-risk proposition and sets you up for a successful second or third sale.

So what if you find that it's been months since you last spoke to a key customer? What if the "champions" who originally decided on your solution are no longer in their original positions?

When things change over time in your customers' worlds, and they will, the ValueSelling conversation can be used again and again to reconnect to the new players and executives in your account. Remember the fundamental ValueSelling Principle: *People need a reason to change.* Now they will need a reason to change away from your company. Proactive communication, review of business issues, uncovering new problems that you are uniquely positioned to address with your solutions are key to customer retention.

Value in the past doesn't necessarily guarantee value in the future. Interestingly enough, once a need has been satisfied or problem has been solved, it is no longer a motivator for us. While that is true, most salespeople don't approach renewal sales with the same rigor of sales process that they do new business. That is a trap that you can avoid with ValueSelling. Use this process for both your renewals and existing customers to ensure that they keep doing business with you and your company.

Practice What You've Learned

At the beginning of this book, I promised you that using the ValueSelling Framework would help you:

- Differentiate your solution and create demand for what you do better than your competitors, while anchoring value for the uniqueness of your solution.

- Increase deal size by minimizing the use of discounts and increasing cross-selling for additional products and services.

- Shorten your sales cycle by simplifying even the most demanding selling situation.

- Deliver higher win rates by more quickly diagnosing the opportunities that are unlikely to close, and freeing your time to focus on opportunities that you are more likely to win.

- Influence your prospects' buying criteria by leveraging your personal credibility and becoming a business advisor or consultant to your prospects, helping them achieve the value of solving their most critical business issues using the products and services supplied by your company.

Have you realized all that value at this point?

As we made clear from the outset, honing your new skill set requires practice. Now that you've taken the first step toward applying the ValueSelling Framework to your customer relationships, you may consider signing up for live follow-up workshops delivered by ValueSelling Associates, where you can further develop your new skills in role-play scenarios.

The following courses complement and enhance what you have learned in this book:

- ValueSelling Online Sales Training is blended learning that incorporates an online self-study course with a companion workshop. Workshops are customized for specific clients and offered to the public.

- eExecutive ValueSelling Online Sales Training prepares the sales executive to have a business conversation with all levels in an organization, especially the decision-making level. This course allows sales executives to build a base of business acumen that provides them with the knowledge and confidence to successfully approach senior business executives and engage them in a business-level conversation.

- Creating Need and Competitive Differentiation are courses that develop the process for developing need and apply it to untapped opportunity.

- Coaching ValueSelling: When implementing organizational change of any kind in a sales organization, the first-line sales managers are critical in the success and sustainability of that change. This workshop develops a coaching model and framework for sales managers of ValueSelling to insure its success.

- Victory! Continuous Improvement for sales professionals. Victory provides just-in-time online training on basic sales competencies. Whether you are trying to better manage your time or negotiate a big deal, Victory has modules that can help you when you need it.

Whether you take additional training courses or try the concepts out with fellow sales associates, using the ValueSelling Framework with a real prospect is where the payoff begins. You may make a few mistakes, but what's the worst that can happen? Your prospect may give you a confused look. Simply restate your question in different words and try, try again!

The point is, if you don't practice the skills you've just learned, you will likely end up reverting to your old ways of doing things, wondering why your sales are stalling. By consistently using the simple, repeatable ValueSelling Framework, you will improve your win rate, grow your deal size and improve your ability to forecast accurately.

Appendix A:
Glossary

Bargaining: A method for gaining direct access to a decision-maker. The tactic is to identify the activities or resources your current contact requires from you and to trade those for access to the decision-maker.

Business Issues: What prospects need to address and resolve to achieve their business objectives.

Business Objectives: What prospects need to accomplish to maintain or grow their business. Most businesses focus on one or more of the following objectives: revenue growth, profitability or market share.

Campaigning: A method for gaining direct access to a decision-maker. The tactic is to uncover the decision-maker's unresolved business issues and then write or call to request a meeting to discuss each unresolved Issue. This method works best if each Issue is addressed separately, giving you several reasons to meet.

Conditional Access: An agreement that guarantees you access to a decision-maker in the event that something goes wrong during your sales effort. Example of a request for Conditional Access: "If my interviews with your staff reveal any situations that might complicate our efforts, or conflict with the direction you have given me, may I bring these matters to your attention for your guidance?"

Confirming Question: A question used to demonstrate that you are listening and understand a prospect's issues. Examples: "So what I heard was … Is that correct?" "Let me see if I heard everything … Did I miss anything?"

Differentiated VisionMatch™: A unique solution that resolves a prospect's business issues and has more value than any competitor's offering.

Modus Operandi: A method for gaining direct access to a decision-maker. The tactic is to state that your mode of operation requires an interview with all the stakeholders impacted by an opportunity. This method works effectively if implemented in the first prospect meetings, but not late in a sales campaign.

Open-Ended Question: A question used to encourage a prospect to expand on a subject. Examples: "Can you tell me why that's a challenge?" "How is that affecting you?"

Paradigm: According to Stephen Covey, author of *The Seven Habits of Highly Effective People*, a unique framework through which an individual views the world. It is formed through a person's education, experience, belief system and value system.

Plan: A proof-of-concept plan that benefits both parties — not an implementation plan. It may be as simple as a letter outlining the set of activities required to bring closure and an agreement between you and your prospect.

Planned Access: An agreement that guarantees you continued access to a decision-maker throughout your sales cycle. The tactic is to identify milestones that justify follow-up meetings with the decision-maker. Examples: meetings to review the findings of your interviews, to review a pricing proposal, or to conduct reference calls together.

Power: The authority to sign off on a project and to allocate money to implement it.

Power Person: The person with the authority to sign off on a project and allocate money to implement it.

Pre-Proposal Review: A meeting with your prospect's buying committee to review your findings and confirm that all the information required to make a decision is in order.

Probing Question: A question used to uncover information about an Issue that you believe might exist in the prospect's organization. The best use of a Probing Question is to pinpoint a problem specific to the prospect's environment or industry that your company resolves better than any competitor can. Examples: "Are you having trouble recruiting skilled people?" "Do you ever run out of materials at critical times?"

Problems: Difficulties that prevent prospects from being able to satisfactorily address or resolve their business issues.

Reverse Timeline: A timeline that starts at a Plan's endpoint and works backward, detailing everything that needs to be accomplished prior to the Plan's completion.

Scope Creep: The addition of requirements for proof beyond the scope of the initial plan.

Triangulation: A research method by which an investigator relies on multiple sources to verify or hone in on the truth.

Value: A prospect's perception of the impact of a solution(s) that resolve(s) their business issue(s). This impact needs to be expressed in terms of business and personal value.

ValueSelling: A framework that includes a set of principles, the ValuePrompter as the dialog framework, and the Qualified Prospect Formula. This will personally differentiate you by helping your prospects see a direct link between their critical business issues and the value of the solutions you have to offer.

VisionMatch: When prospects believe it is possible that the capabilities of the product or service you provide will enable them to solve their problems and resolve their business issues.

Appendix B: Index